# Skills Practice
## Workbook

**Level 3
Book 1**

SRA

*Columbus, OH*

**SRAonline.com**

 **SRA**

Send all inquiries to this address:
SRA/McGraw-Hill
4400 Easton Commons
Columbus, OH 43219-6188

ISBN: 978-0-07-610478-9
MHID: 0-07-610478-8

11 12 13 14 QLM 15 14 13

The McGraw·Hill Companies

# Table of Contents

## Unit 1 Friendship

# Unit 2 Animals and Their Habitats

# Unit 3 Money

Name _____  Date _____

# /ā/, /ē/, /ī/, /ō/, and /ū/ Sound/Spellings

**Focus**
- /ā/ can be spelled a and a_e.
- /ē/ can be spelled e and e_e.
- /ī/ can be spelled i and i_e.
- /ō/ can be spelled o and o_e.
- /ū/ can be spelled u and u_e.

**Practice**  A word is missing in each sentence. Choose the word with the long vowel sound to complete each sentence. Write the word on the blank line.

**1.** A square is a _____ with four sides.
(shape, sharp)

**2.** My dogs like to _____ on my bed.
(lit, lie)

**3.** Put another ice _____ in each glass.
(cub, cube)

**4.** Udu wrote his mother a _____.
(note, not)

**5.** I will _____ there at 4:00.
(bed, be)

**Apply** Read the word in the box. Change the word in the box to make a new rhyming word that completes the sentence. Write the new word on the blank line.

**6.** [ hide ] Moesha likes to _____ her horse, Bo.

**7.** [ toe ] Moesha always wears her riding helmet

_____ her head will be safe.

**8.** [ host ] On _____ school days, they trot around
a field before dinner.

**9.** [ date ] It is so much fun that they _____ having
to stop to eat.

**10.** [ hoe ] She clicks when she wants Bo to _____
and says, "Whoa," to make him stop.

**11.** [ tiny ] Bo has a long, _____ brown mane and
tail.

**12.** [ mute ] Moesha often sings him a _____ song
while she combs his mane.

**13.** [ dime ] Bo and Moesha have been friends for a long

_____.

**14.** [ cute ] Moesha plays the _____ for Bo in
the afternoon.

Name _____     Date _____

# Antonyms and Synonyms

**Antonyms** are words that have opposite meanings. **Synonyms** are words with the same or nearly the same meaning. A dictionary or thesaurus can help you find synonyms for words. Sometimes a dictionary also gives antonyms. A thesaurus often gives antonyms.

Example: loud

Antonyms for *loud:* quiet, silent

Synonyms for *loud:* noisy, deafening, shrill

**Think about the word *grateful* from page 32 of "Rugby & Rosie."**

**1.** Look in a thesaurus or a dictionary. Find two synonyms for the word *grateful.*

_____

**2.** Find an antonym for the word *grateful.*

_____

**3.** Fill in the blanks below with your two synonyms for the word *grateful.* Read each sentence to see if the word makes sense. If the words are synonyms, they should give each sentence a similar meaning.

My friend helped me, and I was grateful.

My friend helped me, and I was _____.

My friend helped me, and I was _____.

**Apply** Find the word *eagerly* on page 20 of "Rugby & Rosie." Read the sentence in which *eagerly* is found. Remember, the context clues in the sentences around the word can help you learn the meaning of the word.

**4.** Write two words that are context clues from the sentence:

_____

**5.** Write two words that you think might be antonyms for the word *eagerly:*

_____

**6.** Write two words that you think might be synonyms for the word *eagerly:*

_____

**7.** Look for *eagerly* in a thesaurus. Find another antonym and another synonym. Think about how they help you understand *eagerly.* Write these words on the lines.

Antonym: _____

Synonym: _____

**8.** Write a new sentence using the word *eagerly*.

_____

_____

# Selection Vocabulary

**Focus**

**chores** (chorz) *n.* plural form of **chore:** a small job (page 18)

**patient** (pā' · shənt) *adj.* willing to wait (page 20)

**ignore** (ig · nor') *v.* to pay no attention to (page 21)

**worried** (wûr' · rēd) *v.* a form of the verb **worry:** to think about troubles (page 22)

**energy** (en' · ûr · jē) *n.* the strength or eagerness to do something (page 24)

**especially** (is · pesh' · el · lē) *adv.* particularly (page 30)

**permission** (pûr · mish' · ən) *n.* when an adult allows one to do something (page 30)

**grateful** (grāt' · fəl) *adj.* thankful (page 32)

**Practice**   Circle the word that matches each sentence.

1. After school Maia has to wash the dishes and take out the trash.

     grateful          chores

2. Jack could not stop thinking about the test tomorrow.

     worried          ignore

3. Omar waited for dinner and did not complain.

     patient          worried

4. "Thank you!" Li said as she opened her present.

     energy          grateful

**Apply**  Match each word on the left to its definition on the right.

**5.** energy

**6.** grateful

**7.** chores

**8.** ignore

**9.** worried

**10.** permission

**11.** patient

**12.** especially

**a.** to pay no attention to

**b.** thankful

**c.** to think about troubles

**d.** willing to wait

**e.** small jobs

**f.** the strength or eagerness to do something

**g.** an adult allowing one to do something

**h.** particularly

**Name** _____ **Date** _____

# Cause and Effect

The **cause** is why something happens. What happens is the **effect.**

When you see words such as *because* and *so,* look for a cause and an effect.

Example: My dog did not eat her food *because* she was not hungry.

**Effect** (What happened?)    The dog did not eat.

**Cause** (Why did it happen?)    The dog was not hungry.

**Practice**    **Read each sentence. Draw a line under the word that shows cause.**

**1.** The door opened because we used the right key.

**2.** The tire was flat, so Paolo could not ride his bike.

**3.** Elephants fan their ears because it cools their blood.

**4.** She was cold, so Ann put on a sweater.

**5.** I went to the store because we were out of milk.

**6.** Nancy liked Jan, so she invited her to the party.

**7.** Ira studied so he would do well on the quiz.

**Apply** Each sentence below shows an effect. What might have caused it? Use the sentence and your own idea to write a new sentence showing cause and effect.

**8.** The eggs cracked. _____

_____

**9.** The tree shook. _____

_____

**10.** My hands are clean. _____

_____

**11.** Carolee fell on the ground. _____

_____

**Each sentence below shows a cause. What might the effect be? Use the sentence and your own idea to write a new sentence showing cause and effect.**

**12.** Dad was using the wrong key. _____

_____

**13.** The ice melted. _____

_____

**14.** The lamp did not work. _____

_____

Name _____ Date _____

# New Ideas and Author Writing Techniques

Each selection in Unit 1 presents you with ideas about friendship. The authors of each selection use writing techniques to share those ideas with you. For each selection, record any new ideas about friendship from the selection. Then, record any writing techniques the author used.

**"Amos & Boris" by William Steig**

New Ideas about Friendship: _____

_____

Writing Techniques: _____

_____

**"Rugby & Rosie" by Nan Parson Rossiter**

New Ideas about Friendship: _____

_____

Writing Techniques: _____

_____

**"The Legend of Damon and Pythias" by Fan Kissen**

New Ideas about Friendship: _____

_____

Writing Techniques: _____

_____

## New Ideas and Author Writing Techniques (continued)

**"Good-bye, 382 Shin Dang Dong" by Frances Park and Ginger Park**

New Ideas about Friendship: _____

_____

_____

Writing Techniques: _____

_____

_____

**"Beauty and the Beast"**

New Ideas about Friendship: _____

_____

_____

Writing Techniques: _____

_____

_____

**"Teammates" by Peter Golenbock**

New Ideas about Friendship: _____

_____

_____

Writing Techniques: _____

_____

Name _____ Date _____

# Writing a List

**Think** **Audience: Who** will read your list?

_____

**Purpose: What** is your reason for making the list?

_____

**Prewriting** Use this graphic organizer to plan your list.

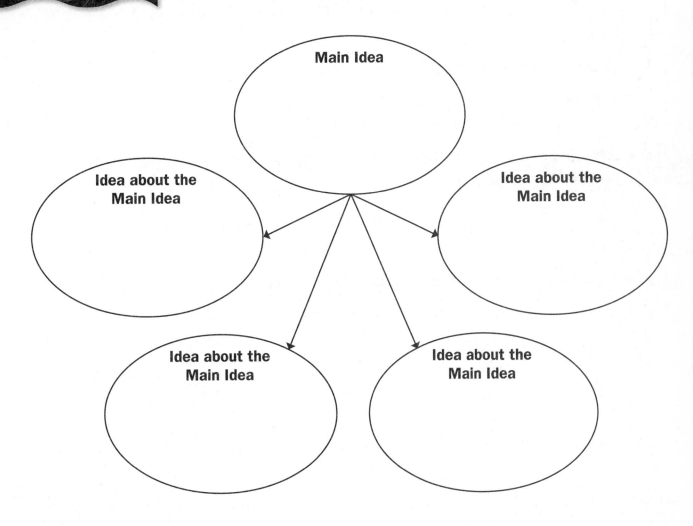

## Revising   Use this checklist to help you revise your list.

☐ Does each item on the list have a number?

☐ Is each item on the list a reason for writing?

☐ Are all your sentences complete?

## Editing/Proofreading   Use this checklist to correct mistakes.

☐ Look at the beginning of each sentence. Did you use a capital letter?

☐ Look at each proper noun. Did you use a capital letter?

☐ Did you use correct spelling?

☐ Did you use the right punctuation?

## Publishing   Use this checklist to prepare a clean copy of your list.

☐ Make sure your list says exactly what you want it to say.

☐ Write neatly or type a final copy of your list.

☐ Read your list for any remaining mistakes.

**Name** _____ **Date** _____

# Spelling

**Focus**

Long vowels sound like their names.

/ā/ spelled a and a_e.

/ē/ spelled e and e_e.

/ī/ spelled i and i_e.

/ō/ spelled o and o_e.

/ū/ spelled u and u_e.

**Practice** Sort the spelling words under the correct heading.

/ā/ spelled a

1. _____

/ā/ spelled a_e

2. _____

3. _____

/ē/ spelled e

4. _____

/ē/ spelled e_e

5. _____

**Word List**

1. tame
2. wild
3. choke
4. wrote
5. music
6. fire
7. blaze
8. menu
9. smile
10. cedar
11. item
12. major
13. cube
14. complete
15. total

**Challenge Words**

16. poem
17. patient
18. grateful

**/ī/ spelled _i_**

6. _____

7. _____

**/ī/ spelled _i_e**

8. _____

9. _____

**/ō/ spelled _o_**

10. _____

**/ō/ spelled _o_e**

11. _____

12. _____

**/ū/ spelled _u_**

13. _____

14. _____

**/ū/ spelled _u_e**

15. _____

**Name** _____ **Date** _____

# Nouns

**Nouns** name a person, place, thing, or idea.

| Rule | Example |
|---|---|
| • Some nouns name a person. | • **Eleanor Roosevelt** helped many people. |
| • Some nouns name a place. | • Someday people will travel to **Mars.** |
| • Some nouns name a thing. | • Danny bought his **saxophone** in California. |
| • Some nouns name an idea. | • **Friendship** makes Gloria and Julian happy. |

**Practice** Write five nouns that name people or things in your classroom and five nouns that name people or things in your home.

Classroom                          Home

_____       _____

_____       _____

_____       _____

_____       _____

_____       _____

**Apply** Tell whether each boldface noun names a person, place, thing, or idea.

**Chicago** _____ is a great **city** _____.

My **neighborhood** _____ is near the **zoo** _____

in **Lincoln Park** _____. **Sophia** _____, my best

**friend** _____, loves to visit me and my **family** _____.

Our favorite animals at the zoo are the **monkeys** _____

and **seals** _____.

**Read this story. Write *yes* if the underlined word
is a noun. Write *no* if the underlined word is not
a noun.**

For _____ the first week of <u>school</u> _____, <u>Lee</u> _____ thought

<u>Yoshi</u> _____ was weird because of what he ate for <u>lunch</u> _____. Yoshi

would <u>come</u> _____ with <u>food</u> _____ Lee had never <u>seen</u> _____

before. <u>Yoshi</u> _____ explained that he came from <u>Japan</u> _____,

where everyone ate that kind of <u>food</u> _____.

**Name** _____ **Date** _____

# Interviewing Guidelines and Questions

**Here are some guidelines to help you with your interview.**

1. **Always ask permission to interview the person.** You can do this face to face, by phone, or by letter. Explain what you are doing and why. Be sure to tell him or her how much time you think you will need.

2. **Decide ahead of time what you want to know.**

3. **Make up questions that will help you get the information you need.**

4. **Write your questions down in an organized order, leaving space between each one for taking notes.**

5. **Speak clearly and be polite.** Pay attention as the person answers.

6. **Take notes on the answers.** Jot down only enough to help you remember what the person said. You might find it helpful to use a tape recorder if one is available. Always ask the person's permission before you record his or her voice.

7. **Read over your notes as soon after you leave the interview as possible, while the conversation is still fresh in your mind.** Make additional notes to help you clarify ideas where necessary.

## Interviewing Guidelines and Questions (continued)

Use these pages to develop questions for your friendship interview. Use the space provided to write questions. Take notes in the Answer spaces during your interview.

**Question:** _____

_____

**Answer:** _____

_____

**Question:** _____

_____

**Answer:** _____

_____

**Question:** _____

_____

**Answer:** _____

_____

**Question:** _____

_____

**Answer:** _____

_____

Name _____ Date _____

# /j/, /s/, /ā/, and /ē/ Sound/Spellings

**Focus**
- /j/ can be spelled *ge* and *gi*.
  Example: *large, giant*
- /s/ can be spelled *ce* and *ci*.
  Example: *face, city*
- Remember, /ā/ can be spelled *a* and *a_e*. /ē/ can be spelled *e* and *e_e*.

**Practice** Read each word below. Write *yes* or *no* to answer the question about the underlined part in each word.

**1.** balance    Is the underlined part an /s/? _____

**2.** giving    Is the underlined part a /j/? _____

**3.** matter    Is the underlined part an /ā/? _____

**4.** general    Is the underlined part a /j/? _____

**5.** meter    Is the underlined part an /ē/? _____

**6.** circle    Is the underlined part an /s/? _____

 **Read each sentence. Choose the correct spelling of the word that completes the sentence. Write the word on the blank line.**

**7.** The Empire State Building is in New York _____.

(Cety, City)

**8.** It was _____ the "Tallest Building in the World."

(named, nam)

**9.** It _____ kept the title for 41 years!

(eeven, even)

**10.** People planned to have airships dock at the building's

_____ spire.

(large, larg)

**11.** But _____ winds made it too dangerous.

(gient, giant)

**12.** At night, colored lights make the building glow from a

_____.

(distanse, distance)

**13.** The color of the lights _____ to match seasons

(chang, change)

and sports events.

**14.** The lights_____ it red, white, and blue for the

(maks, make)

Fourth of July.

Name _____  Date _____

# Compound Words

**Focus**

A **compound word** is a single word formed from two words.

**bird + house = birdhouse** "a *house* for a *bird*"

A compound word can have the same meaning as the two words in it, as in *birdhouse,* or it can have a new meaning.

**cow + boy = cowboy** "*a male who herds cattle*"
(not a *boy* that is a *cow*)

**Practice**

**Read the sentence with the word *heartbroken* on page 47 of "The Legend of Damon and Pythias."**

**1.** Separate the compound word *heartbroken* into its two words:

heartbroken = _____ + _____

**2.** What do you think the compound word *heartbroken* means?

_____

**3.** The word *broken* means "damaged" or "shattered." Look in a dictionary to find out what the word *heart* means.

_____

_____

**4.** The compound word *heartbroken* means "overcome by sorrow." Does it have the exact same meaning as the two words that form it?

_____

**Apply**  Create a compound word from the two given words. Fill in the blanks to define the new compound words.

**5.** head + band = _____

"a _____ worn on the _____"

**6.** sun + shine = _____

"the _____ of a bright _____"

**7.** gold + fish = _____

"a _____-colored _____"

**Find the word *farewell* on page 49 of "The Legend of Damon and Pythias."**

**8.** Look up the definition for the word *fare* as it relates to *well*.

fare: _____

well: a good or kindly manner

**9.** What do you think the word *farewell* means in the sentence?

_____

_____

**10.** Look up *farewell* in a dictionary. Does it match the meaning you

wrote above? _____

Name _____ Date _____

# Selection Vocabulary

**Focus**

**persuaded** (pûr·swād'·əd) *v.* past tense of **persuade:** to convince (page 47)

**curious** (kyur'·ē·əs) *adj.* interested in knowing (page 50)

**exchange** (eks·chānj') *n.* a trade of one thing for another (page 50)

**condition** (kən·dish'·ən) *n.* something needed for another event to happen (page 51)

**deserted** (də·zûrt'·əd) *v.* a form of the verb **desert:** to leave alone (page 53)

**struggled** (stru'·gəld) *v.* past tense of **struggle:** to make a great effort (page 55)

**faith** (fāth) *n.* belief or trust in someone's ability or goodness (page 56)

**miserable** (miz'·ûr·ə·bəl') *adj.* very unhappy (page 56)

**Practice**   **Circle the correct word that best completes each sentence.**

**1.** Sahira gave Nita an apple in _____ for her grapes.

   **a.** exchange      **b.** faith      **c.** condition

**2.** The team felt _____ after losing the game.

   **a.** faith      **b.** curious      **c.** miserable

**3.** The _____ kitten wanted to see what was in the box.

   **a.** curious      **b.** condition      **c.** miserable

**4.** Kim _____ me to go skiing even though I was scared.

   **a.** struggled      **b.** persuaded      **c.** deserted

**Apply**   Tell whether the boldfaced definition that is given for the underlined word in each sentence below makes sense. Circle *Yes* or *No.*

**5.** In a Greek story, a mouse <u>persuaded</u> a lion not to eat him.

**convinced**                                      Yes      No

**6.** "The <u>condition</u> is that I will help you someday," the mouse said.

**something interesting**                          Yes      No

**7.** This idea made the lion <u>curious</u>.

**interested in knowing**                          Yes      No

**8.** "Okay," the lion said. "I will free you in <u>exchange</u> for your promise."

**instead of**                                     Yes      No

**9.** Later, the lion was caught in a trap and was <u>miserable</u>.

**very happy**                                     Yes      No

**10.** He <u>struggled</u> with the ropes, but could not get away.

**traded**                                         Yes      No

**11.** The mouse had not <u>deserted</u> the lion—he came to help.

**to leave alone**                                 Yes      No

**12.** The mouse chewed through the ropes, and rewarded the lion's <u>faith</u>.

**confidence**                                     Yes      No

Name _____ Date _____

# Writing a Friendly Letter

**Think**

**Audience: Who** is the audience for your friendly letter?

_____

**Purpose: What** is your reason for writing this letter?

☐ To share news, stories, and thoughts

☐ To start or continue a friendship

☐ Other _____

**Prewriting**

**Use this graphic organizer to plan your personal letter.**

Heading

Greeting

_____

Body _____

_____

_____

_____  Details

_____

_____

_____

Closing _____

Signature _____

## Revising

**Use this checklist to help you revise your friendly letter. Use proofreading marks to make changes.**

☐ Did you include all of the parts of a friendly letter?

☐ Is there a topic sentence for each paragraph?

☐ Did you use the correct main and helping verbs?

☐ Did you add variety by sometimes using pronouns instead of nouns?

## Editing/Proofreading

**Use this checklist to correct mistakes.**

☐ Are all the names of people and places spelled correctly?

☐ Did you capitalize the greeting and closing?

☐ Did you capitalize the first word of every sentence?

☐ Did you end each sentence with the correct punctuation?

## Publishing

**Use this checklist to help get your letter ready to send.**

☐ Write neatly or type a final copy of your letter.

☐ Add a drawing or photo to your letter.

---

**Proofreading Marks**

¶    New paragraph.

∧    Add something.

⌀    Take out something.

≡    Make a capital letter.

/    Make a lowercase letter.

sp ⟳  Check spelling.

⊙    Add a period.

**Examples**

¶ Once upon a time, years ago, there lived a dinosaur named Rocky. He lived . . .

*shiny*
a⌃penny

Rabbits live in ⌀n burrows.

california
≡

We go camping in ⌀ummer.

sp
(freind)

There are nine planets in the solar system⊙

---

**Name** _____ **Date** _____

# Spelling

**Focus**

A **compound word** is a word made of two smaller words joined together.

/s/ is found in words where the letter c is followed by e, i, or y.

/j/ is found in words where the letter g is followed by e, i, or y.

**Practice**

**Sort the spelling words under their correct heading.**

**Compound words**

1. _____

2. _____

3. _____

4. _____

5. _____

**/s/ spelled ce**

6. _____

7. _____

8. _____

**Word List**

1. shipwreck
2. huge
3. twice
4. homework
5. bulldog
6. gentle
7. range
8. city
9. since
10. notebook
11. decent
12. waterfront
13. germ
14. logic
15. agent

**Challenge Words**

16. exchange
17. garbage
18. distance

**/s/ spelled *ci***

9. _____

**/j/ spelled *ge***

10. _____

11. _____

12. _____

13. _____

14. _____

**/j/ spelled *gi***

15. _____

Name _____ Date _____

# Verbs and Verb Phrases

**Focus**

**Verbs** show the action, condition, or state of being of the subject. There are different types of verbs.

| Rule | Example |
|---|---|
| • **Action verbs** show the actions of the subject. | Sofia **ran.** |
| • **State-of-being verbs** show the condition or state of being of the subject. | I **am** ready to go. |
| • When a state-of-being verb connects the subject with a word in the predicate, it is called a **linking verb.** | He **is** a student. |
| • A **verb phrase** is a verb with two or more words. | Danny **could have flown.** |
| • The last verb in a verb phrase is the **main verb.** | Danny could have **flown.** |
| • **Helping verbs** come before the main verb. | Danny **could have** flown. |

**Practice**

**Read each sentence. Circle *Action Verb* if the sentence has an action verb. Circle *Verb Phrase* if the sentence has a verb phrase.**

**1.** The band played a polka.       Action Verb       Verb Phrase

**2.** Rick has been a jockey.       Action Verb       Verb Phrase

 **Read the paragraph. Circle the action verbs.**

Isadora Duncan wrote a book about herself. She titled it *My Life.* She was a famous modern dancer who taught many children to dance. They happily learned from her. They performed in France, Italy, and Russia.

**Read the paragraph. It is missing some helping verbs. Decide where they should go, and insert them.**

Jamaal singing a solo in the school choir. He has to buy new clothes. He buy a white dress shirt, blue pants, and a red and blue striped tie. His mother will help him pick the clothes. On the day of the concert, he prepared two hours early. His sister asks him if he is nervous. "No," he tells her. "I am ready. I've practiced a lot." Finally, it's time to leave. Jamaal sings very well. His family is proud of him. Afterwards, they going to take him to dinner to celebrate.

Name _____ Date _____

# Choosing Appropriate Sources

**You can use the following sources to find information on a topic.**

| Source | Description |
| --- | --- |
| Atlas | A book of maps that helps you learn about a continent, country, state, or city. Atlases often have information about oceans, rivers, and mountains. |
| Dictionary | A reference book containing an alphabetical list of words that includes spelling, meaning, and pronunciation. |
| Thesaurus | A reference book containing an alphabetical list of synonyms. |
| Encyclopedia | A set of reference books that contains general information on many subjects. These subjects are in alphabetical order. |
| Magazines, Newspapers | These "periodicals" come out daily, weekly, monthly, or several times a year. Current issues contain up-to-date information. |
| Nonfiction Books | Nonfiction books provide facts about a topic or group of topics. |
| Interview | A planned conversation with a person who is an expert on a topic. |
| Museums and Organizations | These institutions provide information on subjects through exhibits, displays, and experts you can interview. |
| Internet | A network of Web sites with information on a wide range of topics. |

## Choosing Appropriate Sources (continued)

**Use the list of sources on the previous page to decide where to look for the information. Write the best choice or choices on the line.**

**1.** Where is Vietnam located?

_____

**2.** How does electricity work?

_____

**3.** What is the definition of *cooperation?*

_____

**4.** What damage was caused by the storm last night?

_____

**5.** Who was elected governor of our state during the last election?

_____

**6.** Where was President Lincoln born and when was he elected president?

_____

**7.** What is another word that has the same meaning as the word *friendship?*

_____

**Name** _____ **Date** _____

# /ā/, /ē/, /ī, /ō/, /ū/, /j/, and /s/ Sound/Spellings

**Focus**
- Remember, /ā/ can be spelled *a* and *a_e*. /ē/ can be spelled *e* and *e_e*. /ī/ can be spelled *i* and *i_e*. /ō/ can be spelled *o* and *o_e*. /ū/ can be spelled *u* and *u_e*.

- /**j**/ can be spelled *j* and *dge*.
  Example: *ju<u>dge</u>*

- /**s**/ can be spelled *s* and *cy*.
  Examples: *<u>s</u>oft, <u>cy</u>cle*

**Practice**    **Read each word below. Circle *Yes* if the word has a /j/ or an /s/ sound. Circle *No* if it does not.**

**1.** fudge          Yes          No

**2.** simple          Yes          No

**3.** colander          Yes          No

**4.** dodging          Yes          No

**5.** degree          Yes          No

**6.** coyly          Yes          No

**Apply** Sometimes words at the end of a poem's lines will rhyme. Write a word from the box to complete each rhyme below.

| | | |
|---|---|---|
| joy | glide | may |
| be | edge | crime |

**7.** Surfers will take a surfboard for a ride.

The force of the water allows them to _____.

**8.** Afloat in the water they're happy to _____,

Waiting for waves that roll in from the sea.

**9.** Part of the trick is to catch each in time.

To miss a great wave sometimes feels like a _____.

**10.** A surfer pops up on the board's slippery _____,

And rides down the wave on its white, foamy ledge.

**11.** The rush of the wave! The crazy, free _____!

On the huge, open sea, the board's like a small toy.

**12.** Once the wave's over, the surfer will stay.

A better wave's coming. It might be. It _____.

Name _____ Date _____

# Contractions

**Focus**

A **contraction** is a word formed from two or more words. Some letters are left out when the words combine.

An apostrophe (') marks the spot where the letters were dropped.

- Some contractions look the same, but mean different things. For example, *he'd* can mean "he had" <u>or</u> "he would."

- Only one contraction, *I'm*, is made with the word *am*. Only one contraction, *let's*, is made with the word *us*.

**Practice**

Write the words that combine to make each contraction. Some contractions can be made by two sets of words.

**1.** she'll _____ + _____

**2.** I'd _____ + _____

_____ + _____

**3.** can't _____ + _____

**4.** you'll _____ + _____

**5.** we'd _____ + _____

_____ + _____

**6.** didn't _____ + _____

**Apply**   **Read each sentence below. Circle the pair or pairs of words that can be made into contractions. Write each contraction on a line.**

**7.** Ling and I decided we would like to go sledding.

_____

**8.** Since it is cold outside, we will have to put on warm coats.

_____   _____

**9.** We are going to call some friends to see if they will come, too.

_____   _____

**10.** There is lots of snow on the ground, so it is going to be a fun day.

_____   _____

**In the letter below, the writer made some mistakes writing contractions. Cross out each mistake. Write the correct contraction in the margin.**

Dear Grandmother,

How are you? Im fine. I am enjoying my visit to Ireland.

Yesterday I saw the Cliffs of Moher. Theyr'e tall cliffs. You

cann't get too close, or the wind will knock you down!

Today I's going to have lunch in the city of Galway.

Maybe today I'will have the seafood stew.

Love,

Margaret

Name _____ Date _____

# Selection Vocabulary

**Focus**

**foreign** (for'·ən) *adj.* of or from another country (page 67)

**assure** (əsh·ûr') *v.* to make certain or sure (page 68)

**pastel** (pas·tel') *adj.* a pale, soft shade of a color (page 70)

**glum** (glum) *adj.* very unhappy or disappointed (page 71)

**enthusiastic** (en·thoo'·zē·ast'·ik) *adj.* very excited about something (page 73)

**peculiar** (pi·kūl'·yər) *adj.* not usual; strange (page 74)

**translation** (tranz·lā'·shən) *n.* a changing of a speech or piece of writing into another language (page 76)

**insisted** (in·sist'·əd) *v.* past tense of **insist:** demand or say in a strong, firm manner (page 76)

**Practice** **Tell whether the boldfaced definition for the underlined word makes sense. Circle *Yes* or *No.***

**1.** Tano read a <u>translation</u> of *The Little Prince.*

**a piece of writing changed into another language**  Yes  No

**2.** I felt <u>glum</u> when the picnic was rained out.

**very unhappy**  Yes  No

**3.** The baby <u>insisted</u> she was hungry by crying loudly.

**to make sure**  Yes  No

**Apply** Circle the correct word that completes each sentence.

**4.** I just got a _____ of a letter from my Italian pen pal.

   **a.** pastel     **b.** translation     **c.** foreign

**5.** Mia _____ that I should visit her in Italy.

   **a.** insisted     **b.** assured     **c.** glum

**6.** She will feel _____ if I can't come see her.

   **a.** glum     **b.** enthusiastic     **c.** assure

**7.** Her family would be excited to have a _____ visitor.

   **a.** pastel     **b.** glum     **c.** foreign

**8.** She _____ me that I would like *confetti*.

   **a.** translation     **b.** assured     **c.** enthusiastic

**9.** *Confetti* is nut colored with a _____ coating.

   **a.** translation     **b.** enthusiastic     **c.** pastel

**10.** The name *confetti* seems _____ to me.

   **a.** peculiar     **b.** glum     **c.** translation

**11.** Her town is known for this treat, so she is _____.

   **a.** foreign     **b.** translation     **c.** enthusiastic

Name _____ Date _____

# Author's Point of View

**Focus**

Every story is told from a point of view.

• When a story is told by a character, the story is told in the **first-person point of view.** The clue words *I* and *we* are used.

• When a story is told by the author, the story is told in the **third-person point of view.** The clue words *she, he,* and *they* are used.

**Practice**

**Look through "Good-bye, 382 Shin Dang Dong" for an example of a sentence that shows point of view. Write it below. Then, answer the questions.**

**1.** Page: _____

Sentence: _____

_____

_____

**2.** From what point of view is the story told? _____

_____

**3.** How did you decide from what point of view the story is told?

_____

_____

_____

 Read the paragraph that follows. Decide whether it is written in the first-person or third-person point of view. Explain your answer.

Tamika got a new bike for her birthday. Her brother, Dwayn, offered to show her how to ride. Dwayn told Tamika that the first thing she had to do was learn how to ride safely. He gave Tamika a helmet and showed her how to put it on. He also helped her attach training wheels to the bike. When he was finished, he told Tamika to hop on while he walked along beside her.

**4.** What is the point of view of the paragraph? _____

_____

**5.** How do you know the point of view? _____

_____

_____

**Rewrite the paragraph above from another point of view.**

_____

_____

_____

_____

_____

**Name** _____ **Date** _____

# Fantasy Story

 **Think**   **Audience: Who** will read your fantasy story?

_____

**Purpose: What** is your reason for writing a make-believe story?

_____

**Prewriting**   Use this graphic organizer to plan your fantasy story.

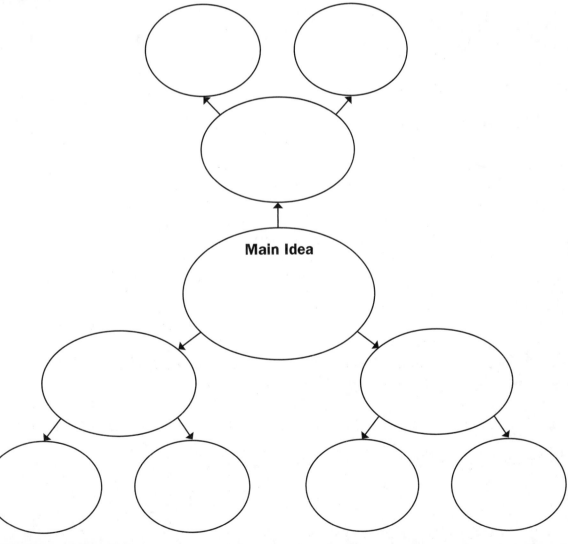

## Revising  Use this checklist to revise your fantasy story.

- ☐ Did you begin your sentences in different ways?
- ☐ Did you use one point of view?
- ☐ Do you describe the setting so readers feel like they are there?
- ☐ Does your story have a problem that is solved?
- ☐ Do your events happen in an order that makes sense?
- ☐ Did you add descriptive detail?

## Editing/Proofreading  Use this checklist to correct mistakes.

- ☐ Did you use correct spelling?
- ☐ Did you use capital letters at the beginning of each sentence?
- ☐ Did you end each sentence with correct punctuation?
- ☐ Do all your subjects and verbs agree?
- ☐ Did you use commas in lists with three or more adjectives?

## Publishing  Use this checklist to finish the first draft of your fantasy story.

- ☐ Neatly rewrite or type a final copy.
- ☐ Save your story and continue to revise.

Name _____  Date _____

# Spelling

**Focus** **Contractions** are words formed from two words. Some letters are left out when the two words combine and an apostrophe (') marks the spot where the letters were dropped.

**Long vowels** sound like their names.

/ā/ can be spelled a and a_e.

/ē/ can be spelled e and e_e.

/ī/ can be spelled i and i_e.

/ō/ can be spelled o and o_e.

/ū/ can be spelled u and u_e.

/s/ is usually found in words where the letter c is followed by e, i, or y.

**Practice** Sort the spelling words under the correct heading.

**Contractions**

1. _____

2. _____

3. _____

4. _____

5. _____

**Word List**

1. she'd
2. we'll
3. haven't
4. wasn't
5. aren't
6. would've
7. doesn't
8. that's
9. page
10. cube
11. moment
12. strike
13. basic
14. human
15. cellar

**Challenge Words**

16. o'clock
17. shouldn't

**6.** _____

**7.** _____

**8.** _____

*/ā/* spelled *a_e*

**9.** _____

*/ū/* spelled *u_e*

**10.** _____

*/ō/* spelled *o*

**11.** _____

*/ī/* spelled *i_e*

**12.** _____

*/ā/* spelled *a*

**13.** _____

*/ū/* spelled *u*

**14.** _____

*/s/* spelled *ce*

**15.** _____

Name _____ Date _____

# Subject and Predicate

**Focus**

| Rule | Example |
|---|---|
| • The **simple subject** names who or what the sentence is about. It is usually a noun or pronoun. | • My **mother** is a doctor. **She** works at the hospital. |
| • A **compound subject** has two or more simple subjects combined by a conjunction. | • **Tyrone** and **I** went horseback riding. |
| • A **simple predicate** tells what the subject is or does. | • My daughter **visits** her grandmother once a month. |
| • A **compound predicate** shows two or more things about the same subject. They are connected by a conjunction. | • The zebras **eat** and **sleep** at the zoo. |

**Practice**    Write *S* for simple or *C* for compound for the subject on the first line and for the predicate on the second line.

**1.** Abraham Lincoln was born in 1809. ___, ___

**2.** Lincoln and his parents first lived in Kentucky. ___, ___

**3.** Lincoln was elected president in 1860. ___, ___

**4.** He wrote many important speeches. ___, ___

**5.** Lincoln lived and worked in Washington, D.C. ___, ___

**Apply**   Change the sentence fragments below into sentences by adding subjects and predicates.

**6.** Estelle _____ at the supermarket.

**7.** The supermarket _____ at 7 A.M.

**8.** _____ arrives at work at 6:30 A.M.

**9.** _____ and _____ work with Estelle.

**10.** They _____ at 6:30 A.M. also.

**11.** Estelle _____ and _____ the floors before opening.

**12.** _____ and _____ wash the windows before opening.

**Circle the subjects and underline the simple predicates.**

Many immigrants lived in Cincinnati in the 1800s. Their neighborhood was called Over-the-Rhine. Many of them could not afford a house. Working together, they formed associations to save money and build homes. They each gave money every week, and when they had enough money, they held a drawing. The association used everyone's money to build a home for the winner.

Name _____ Date _____

# ABC Order

ABC order, or alphabetical order, is a good way to organize lists. Look at the first letter of each word and arrange the words in ABC order. If the first letters are the same, use the letter or letters that follow them: *stem, stick, stump*.

Use the lines below to write down the first names of all of the students in your class. Then on the next page, write the list of names in ABC order.

_____     _____

_____     _____

_____     _____

_____     _____

_____     _____

_____     _____

_____     _____

_____     _____

_____     _____

## ABC Order (continued)

**Names in ABC order:**

_____

_____

_____

_____

_____

_____

_____

_____

_____

_____

**Name** _____ **Date** _____

# /ā/, /ē/, and Consonant Blends Sound/Spellings

**Focus**

- **/ā/** can be spelled *ai_* and *_ay*.
  Example: *afr<u>ai</u>d, ma<u>y</u>*

- **/ē/** can be spelled *ea, ee, _ie, _y,* and *_ey*.
  Example: *b<u>ea</u>n, s<u>ee</u>n, bel<u>ie</u>ve, luck<u>y</u>, mon<u>ey</u>*

- **Consonant blends** can be at the beginning or end of words.
  Example: *<u>bl</u>end, <u>sp</u>ark; dam<u>p</u>, bes<u>t</u>*

**Practice**  Circle the word in each pair with the correct /ā/ or /ē/ sound spelling.

**1.** payd      paid

**2.** hony      honey

**3.** feed      fead

**4.** lieve      leave

**5.** stray      strai

**6.** happee      happy

**7.** team      tiem

**8.** away      awaiy

**Apply** Write the correct word to complete each sentence.

**9.** There is an Eastern African story about a _____ of rats.
(grump, group)

**10.** They used to _____ into a big house to get food.
(sneak, snake)

**11.** However, the big cat in the house would always _____
(chase, cheese)
them.

**12.** "Brothers and sisters," said one rat to the others, "we must solve

this _____."
(problem, pressed)

**13.** So they built a _____, strong hole in a wall.
(smell, small)

**14.** The cat could not get _____ it, but they could!
(throw, through)

**15.** But one rat said, "The cat can still _____ us when we
(snore, snatch)
come from the hole."

**16.** "Who will tie a bell _____ the cat's neck so we will hear him?"
(found, around)
she asked.

**17.** Every rat was _____; they were all afraid.
(spent, silent)

**18.** Everyone liked the idea, but only one was willing to take the

_____.
(whisk, risk)

Name _____ Date _____

# Related Words

**Focus** **Related words** are words that could be found in the same grouping.

Example:

- The words *nest, eggs,* and *seed* all relate to birds.
- The words *tire, windshield,* and *trunk* all relate to cars.

**Practice** **Read each set of words below. Cross out the word that is not related to the others.**

| | | | | |
|---|---|---|---|---|
| **1.** stir | cook | recipe | swing | ingredients |
| **2.** cousin | family | job | sister | aunt |
| **3.** ideas | create | design | imagine | necklace |
| **4.** actor | athlete | sports | compete | game |
| **5.** travel | adventure | explore | tourist | repair |
| **6.** doctor | treatment | medical | mountain | hospital |

 **Apply** Read each sentence below. Decide which word from the box is related to the underlined word. Write the word on the line.

| | | | |
|---|---|---|---|
| lava | car | calendar | trip |
| fire | antlers | plant | fog |

**7.** My family just went on <u>vacation</u> to Yellowstone National Park.

_____

**8.** It was a long <u>drive</u>, but it was worth it. _____

**9.** Right after we drove in, we saw <u>elk</u> eating grass in a field.

_____

**10.** We hiked to see some geysers, which are holes that blast <u>steam</u>

and water. _____

**11.** Fog hung over the <u>grass</u>, and the air smelled strange.

_____

**12.** I found out that part of the park is a very old <u>volcano</u>.

_____

**13.** The <u>heat</u> that's still underground makes the geysers steam and spray.

_____

**14.** Yellowstone is so big that I told Mom we have to go again next <u>year</u>!

_____

Name _____  Date _____

# Selection Vocabulary

**Focus**

**magnificent** (mag·nif'·is·ənt') *adj.* very beautiful and grand; splendid (page 92)

**flattered** (fla'·tərd) *v.* a form of the verb **flatter:** to praise too much without meaning it (page 94)

**mercy** (mûr'·sē) *n.* kindness or forgiveness greater than what is expected or deserved (page 94)

**clung** (klung) *v.* past tense of **cling:** to stick closely (page 96)

**timidly** (tim'·id·lē) *adv.* in a way that shows shyness or a lack of courage (page 98)

**sighed** (sīd) *v.* past tense of **sigh:** to make a long, deep breathing sound because of sadness, tiredness, or relief (page 99)

**despair** (də·spâr') *n.* a complete loss of hope (page 101)

**splendor** (splen'·dûr) *n.* a great display, as of riches or beautiful objects (page 103)

**Practice**  **Match the vocabulary words with their synonyms.**

**1.** mercy

**2.** clung

**3.** flattered

**4.** timidly

**5.** sighed

**6.** magnificent

**a.** moaned

**b.** compassion

**c.** nervously

**d.** held

**e.** grand

**f.** praised

**Apply** Use the clues to complete the crossword puzzle below.

**Across**

**7.** breathed out loudly
**9.** very beautiful
**11.** a feeling of no hope
**12.** undeserved kindness
**13.** stayed very close

**Down**

**7.** a sight that is beautiful
**8.** gave too much praise
**10.** done in a shy way

Name _____ Date _____

# Interview Questions and Answers

Use these pages to write questions about friendship that you want to ask in an interview. When you give your interview, listen carefully to the answers and record them here.

**Question:** _____

_____

**Answer:** _____

_____

_____

**Question:** _____

_____

**Answer:** _____

_____

_____

**Question:** _____

_____

**Answer:** _____

_____

_____

## Interview Questions and Answers (continued)

**Question:** _____

_____

**Answer:** _____

_____

_____

**Question:** _____

_____

**Answer:** _____

_____

_____

**Question:** _____

_____

**Answer:** _____

_____

_____

**Name** _____ **Date** _____

# Spelling

**Focus** **Related words** are words that have a similar theme.

**Long vowels** sound like their names.

/ā/ can be spelled *ai_* and *_ay*.

/ē/ can be spelled *ea*, *_y*, *ee*, *_ie_*, and *_ey*.

**Consonant blends** are groups of two or three consonants in which the sound of each letter can be heard.

**Practice** Sort the spelling words under the correct heading.

**Related words**

1. _____ _____

2. _____ _____ _____

**Consonant blends at the beginning with /ā/**

3. _____

4. _____

5. _____

**Consonant blends at the beginning with /ē/**

6. _____

7. _____

**Word List**

1. mercy
2. heavy
3. spray
4. honey
5. brief
6. field
7. street
8. alley
9. plain
10. turkey
11. east
12. day
13. week
14. year
15. claim

**Challenge Words**

16. timidly
17. despair

**Consonant blends at the end**

8. _____

9. _____

**Remaining words with /ē/**

10. _____

11. _____

12. _____

13. _____

Name _____  Date _____

# Complete Simple Sentence

**Focus** A **complete simple sentence** has one subject and one predicate.

| Rule | Example |
|------|---------|
| • The **subject** can be simple or compound. | • Henry skates. *or* Henry and Eben skate. |
| • The **predicate** can be simple or compound. | • Henry skates. *or* Henry skates and glides. |
| • One sentence can have a **compound subject** and a **compound predicate.** | • Henry and Eben skate and glide. |
| • A simple sentence can be very long. | • Henry and Eben skate and glide across the smooth, shining ice for hours. |

**Practice** Decide whether each sentence below has a simple or compound subject. Write *simple* or *compound.*

1. Whales are interesting mammals. _____

2. Krill and small fish are the food of many whales. _____

3. The biggest animal on earth is the blue whale. _____

4. Shortfin pilot whales and killer whales are the fastest swimmers.

_____

**Apply**  Decide whether each sentence below has a simple or compound predicate. Write *simple* or *compound.*

**5.** Manatees also live in the ocean. _____

**6.** These mammals move and swim slowly. _____

**7.** Its flippers and tail move it through the water. _____

**8.** Manatees swim up and breathe. _____

**Read each pair of sentences below. Rewrite them so they are one sentence with a compound subject, a compound predicate, or both.**

**9.** I have a pet hamster named Philip. My sister shares Philip, too.

_____

_____

**10.** Philip runs on a wheel. Philip drinks from a bottle.

_____

_____

**11.** Philip likes hamster food. Philip eats hamster food.

_____

_____

**12.** My sister and I play with Philip. We clean his cage.

_____

_____

Name _____ Date _____

# Following Directions

**Focus** Directions tell you how to do something or go somewhere. When you **follow directions,** you follow the directions in order.

**Practice** Read the following set of directions. Answer the questions below.

---

**How to Plant a Garden**

1. Find a good spot where your garden will get about six hours of sunlight a day.
2. Dig and break up the dirt in your garden space.
3. Dig a hole for each seed or plant. Leave space between each hole so the plants have room to grow.
4. Place a seed or seedling in each hole.
5. Fill in the hole with loose dirt.
6. Water your seeds or seedlings every other day.
7. Watch your garden grow.

---

**1.** What are these directions telling about?

_____

**2.** What would you do before you plant each seed?

_____

**3.** What would you do after you plant each seed?

_____

**4.** What is the last thing you do?

**Apply** Look at the map below. Read the directions from Lauren's house to her new school. Follow the directions by drawing her route on the map below.

Lauren's House →

Maple Ave.

Oak St.

Carson St.

Bluebird St.

Ivy Ave.

Poplar Ave.

Lauren's School

**5.** Start at Lauren's house.

**6.** Turn right on Oak St. Go past Maple Ave.

**7.** Turn left on Ivy Ave.

**8.** Turn right on Carson St.

**9.** Turn left on Poplar Ave.

**10.** Follow Poplar Ave past Bluebird St. Your new school is on the right.

Name _____ Date _____

# /f/, /m/, /n/, /r/, Review of Long Vowels and Consonant Blends

**Focus**

Sometimes consonants combine to make new sounds.

• *ph* combine to make **/f/**

• *_mb* combine to make **/m/**

• *kn_* combine to make **/n/**

• *wr_* combine to make **/r/**

Remember the sound spellings you learned in this unit:

• Long vowels **/ā/, /ē/, /ī/, /ō/, /ū/.**

• */j/* spelled *ge, gi, dge,* and *j;* **/s/** spelled *ce, ci, s,* and *cy.*

• **Consonant blends** are pairs of letters such as *tr* or *mp.* They can be at the beginning or end of words.

**Practice**

Read each word. Write *Yes* if it has the /f/, /m/, /n/, or /r/ sound as shown in the Focus box above. Write *No* if it does not. Circle the letters that spell these sounds.

**1.** fruit _____

**2.** graph _____

**3.** knife _____

**4.** ring _____

**5.** crumb _____

**6.** wrist _____

**7.** knocked _____

**8.** lamb _____

**Apply**    Circle the correct spelling to complete each sentence.

9. People have _____ different things as money.

   uesd            used

10. Whale teeth were _____ as a prize on Fiji islands.

    nown            known

11. In lots of countries, people paid with cows and _____.

    lams            lambs

12. People _____ their names on paper to pay off debts.

    wrote           rote

13. The first banks were _____ places to keep grain.

    central         sentral

14. In ancient Rome, soldiers' _____ were salt.

    wages           wadges

15. Some Russian people used pieces of sheepskin as small

    "_____."

    shange          change

16. _____ people in the world used shells like coins.

    Many            Maney

Name _____    Date _____

# Review of Antonyms, Synonyms, Compound Words, Contractions, and Related Words

**Focus**    Remember what you have learned in Unit 1.

| Types of Words | Examples |
| --- | --- |
| • **Antonyms** are words with opposite meanings. | • hate, love |
| • **Synonyms** are words that mean the same or nearly the same thing. | • toss, throw |
| • A **compound word** is a single word formed from two words. | • bird + house = birdhouse |
| • A **contraction** is another word formed from two words. In a contraction, some of the letters are dropped, and an apostrophe is used. | • do + not = don't |
| • **Related words** are words that can be grouped together. | • *Poodle, leash,* and *paw* are all words that relate to dogs. |

**Practice**    **Read each pair of words. If they can form a compound word, write it on the line. If they can form a contraction, write it on the line.**

**1.** she        would        _____

**2.** down       pour         _____

**3.** her        self         _____

**Apply** Decide whether each word pair are synonyms, antonyms, or related words. Write your answer on the line.

**4.** understand     know     _____

**5.** rain     hail     _____

**6.** test     study     _____

**7.** awake     asleep     _____

**8.** unhappy     sad     _____

**Read each sentence below. Cross out the underlined word. Write an antonym that makes more sense.**

**9.** Joe found his shoes because he <u>forgot</u> where he had put them.

_____

**10.** The kite soared <u>low</u> up in the air.

_____

**11.** My legs sank up to my knees in the <u>shallow</u> mud!

_____

**12.** The <u>quiet</u> crowd screamed and cheered.

_____

Name _____ Date _____

# Selection Vocabulary

**Focus**

**leagues** (lēgz) *n.* plural form of **league**: a group of teams (page 113)

**challenge** (chal'·lənj) *v.* to question the truth of (page 115)

**compete** (kəm·pēt') *v.* to try to win (page 115)

**opponents** (əp·pō'·nəntz) *n.* plural form of **opponent**: a person on the other side (page 116)

**possess** (pəz·zes') *v.* to have; to own (page 116)

**series** (sē'·rēz) *pl. n.* several in a row (page 117)

**responded** (rə·spônd'·əd) *v.* past tense of **respond**: to answer (page 119)

**equal** (ē'·kwəl) *n.* someone who is at the same level as others (page 120)

**Practice** Draw a line connecting each vocabulary word with its synonym.

**1.** responded

**2.** compete

**3.** possess

**4.** leagues

**5.** challenge

**6.** opponents

**a.** have

**b.** enemies

**c.** question

**d.** reacted

**e.** fight

**f.** groups

**Apply**   **Circle the vocabulary word that best completes each sentence below.**

**7.** Martin Luther King Jr. is famous for _____
(possessing, challenging)
segregation.

**8.** His wife, however, was part of the same _____
(opponents, league)
of heroes.

**9.** After King was killed, Coretta Scott King kept fighting for

_____ rights.
(series, equal)

**10.** That sad _____ of events did not slow her down.
(series, league)

**11.** Just four days after his death, she _____ by
(responded, competed)
leading a huge march.

**12.** She fought his _____, and started a center in
(series, opponents)
King's name.

**13.** This center _____ many books and teaching
(possesses, challenges)
tools.

**14.** Instead of _____ with his fame, she helped it
(responding, competing)
live on.

Name _____ Date _____

# Main Idea and Supporting Details

**Focus**

The **main idea** is what the story or paragraph is mostly about. **Supporting details,** or other bits of information, help tell more about the main idea.

| **Main Idea** | **Example** |
| --- | --- |
| • Often the main idea will be the first or last sentence in a paragraph. | • _It was a bad day._ |
| • Supporting details help readers understand the main idea. | • _It was a bad day. I lost my backpack. Then we had a pop quiz in math. When it was time to go home, I missed the bus!_ |

**Practice**

Read each list of details. Then, write the main idea to fit each list.

**1.** _to cool off_      _to build sand castles_

     _to swim_      _to have fun in the sun_

The main idea: _____

**2.** _get presents_      _blow out the candles_

     _play games_      _sing a special song_

The main idea: _____

**Apply** Look through "Teammates" for main-idea sentences that are followed by details. Write one example, and then list the details that tell more about the main idea.

**3.** Page: _____

Main Idea: _____

_____

Details about the main idea: _____

_____

_____

**Read each main-idea sentence below. Write two more sentences that give supporting details.**

**4.** Dad decided to wash the car.

Detail sentence: _____

Detail sentence: _____

**5.** It was the perfect fall day.

Detail sentence: _____

Detail sentence: _____

Name _____ Date _____

# Autobiography

**Think**

**Audience: Who** will read your autobiography?

_____

_____

**Purpose: What** is your reason for writing the autobiography?

_____

_____

**Prewriting**

**Use this graphic organizer to plan your autobiography.**

☐ Think of important things that have happened to you. Write them under the line.

☐ Think of years that go with each event. Write them on top of the line.

**Timeline**

Date:

Event:

## Revising
**Use this checklist to revise your ideas for your autobiography.**

- ☐ Are your events in correct time order?
- ☐ Will your events show your life?
- ☐ Are there more events you could add?
- ☐ Do you show your main idea for each paragraph clearly?
- ☐ Will your main idea make someone want to read on?

## Editing/Proofreading
**Use this checklist to correct mistakes.**

- ☐ Did you use correct spelling?
- ☐ Look at each proper noun. Did you use a capital letter?
- ☐ Did you write dates correctly?
- ☐ Did you use correct punctuation?
- ☐ Do your subjects and verbs agree?
- ☐ Did you indent the first line of each paragraph?

## Publishing
**Use this checklist to finish writing your autobiography.**

- ☐ Neatly rewrite or type a final copy.
- ☐ Read to check for any remaining mistakes.
- ☐ Save your autobiography to use later.

Name _____  Date _____

# Spelling

**Focus**

**kn_** at the beginning of a word makes the /n/ sound.

**wr_** at the beginning of a word makes the /r/ sound.

**ph** makes the /f/ sound.

**mb** makes the /m/ sound.

**Practice**  Sort the spelling words under the correct heading.

### /n/ spelled kn_

1. _____

2. _____

3. _____

4. _____

### /r/ spelled wr_

5. _____

6. _____

7. _____

### /f/ spelled ph

8. _____

9. _____

**Word List**

1. knot
2. write
3. phony
4. climb
5. knee
6. graph
7. phase
8. know
9. wreath
10. thumb
11. wrist
12. lamb
13. trophy
14. knife
15. comb

**Challenge Words**

16. dolphin
17. wrestle
18. triumph

10. _____

11. _____

**/m/ spelled *mb***

12. _____

13. _____

14. _____

15. _____

**Name** _____ **Date** _____

# Quotation Marks, Commas, and Capitalization

**Quotations marks** show when someone is speaking, and they can set off the titles of short pieces of writing, like short stories.

- Use quotation marks before and after the words of a speaker.

- "That doctor is a quack," said the duck.

- Use quotation marks before and after the titles of short stories, poems, songs, and chapters of books.

- We read the poem "Janey" in class.

Use a **comma** to separate a speaker's words from the rest of the sentence.

- The comma goes inside the quotation marks.

- "Do not cross the street," Mr. Shabazz said.

**Capitalize** titles of movies, plays, and television shows. Capitalize the first word of a speaker or a quotation.

- The main words of a title are capitalized. Words like *of*, *the*, and *on* are lowercase.

- I read the short story "**S**un **o**n **t**he **S**and."

- Capitalize a speaker's first word.

- He said, "**T**he boat is too slow."

**Write *yes* if the quotation marks and comma are used correctly. Write *no* if the quotation marks and comma are not used correctly.**

**1.** "I can fly over the tallest building, said the hawk. _____

**2.** "I can sit on the highest building ledge," the eagle said. _____

**3.** People feed me bits of bread all day," said the pigeon. _____

**4.** "I just sit inside and sing" said the canary. _____

**Apply** Put quotation marks around the poem titles in these sentences. Underline three times letters that should be capitalized. (Hint: Remember, words like *and, the,* and *of* are capitalized only if they are the first word.)

**5.** I like the poem one inch tall by Shel Silverstein.

**6.** where the Sidewalk ends is another good poem by Silverstein.

**7.** Jack Prelutsky wrote the poem bleezer's ice cream.

**8.** In Bleezer's ice Cream, an ice cream man sells crazy flavors.

**9.** But the best silly poem is alligator Dance, which I wrote!

**Add quotation marks where needed.**

"What is spring? the city squirrel said to the raccoon.

What do you mean?" the raccoon asked.

The squirrel said, "I mean, I hear other animals talk about spring. But all I see are buildings, cars, and people."

Once you really look for spring," the raccoon said, "you will see it. You will see robins' eggs, wildflowers, and, of course, animals like us.

"Hmm," said the squirrel. "I guess I'll go look for spring."

**Name** _____ **Date** _____

# Parts of a Book

**Knowing the parts of a book can help a reader locate information quickly and easily. Use the information below to answer the questions on the next page.**

### Title page
- appears at the beginning of the book.
- gives the title of the book, the name of the author or editor, and the name of the publisher.

### Copyright page
- appears after the title page.
- gives the publisher's name and the place and year in which the book was published.

### Table of contents
- appears in the front of the book.
- lists units, chapters, or stories, along with their page numbers.
- lists materials in the same order that they appear in the book.

### Glossary
- appears in the back of the book.
- alphabetically lists new words used in the book with their definitions.

### Bibliography
- appears in the back of the book.
- alphabetically lists books or articles the author used.

### Index
- appears in the back of the book.
- alphabetically lists names, places, and topics in the book, with page numbers.

## Parts of a Book (continued)

**1.** Where would you look to find out what year the

book was published? _____

**2.** Where would you look to find how many chapters

the book has? _____

**3.** Where would you look to find the definition of a

word from the book? _____

**4.** Where would you look to find out what books the

author used to find information? _____

**5.** Where would you look to find the title of the book?

_____

**6.** Where would you look to see if the book has

information about birds? _____

**Look in your other textbooks to see how many parts
you can locate for each.**

Name _____  Date _____

# /ī/ Sound Spellings and Consonant Blends

**Focus**
- /ī/ can be spelled *igh* at the end or in the middle of words. Example: s<u>igh</u>, n<u>igh</u>t
- /ī/ can also be spelled *ie* or *y* at the end of a word. Example: t<u>ie</u>, sk<u>y</u>
- Remember: **consonant blends** are pairs of consonants in which you can hear each letter's sound. They are usually at the beginning or at the end of words. Example: <u>tr</u>uck, <u>spl</u>ash

**Practice**  Read each word. Write *long i* if the word has /ī/. Write *blend* if it begins or ends with a consonant blend. Write *neither* if it has neither.

**1.** given  _____

**2.** higher  _____

**3.** lies  _____

**4.** thigh  _____

**5.** brick  _____

**6.** funny  _____

**Apply**   Choose a word from the box to complete each sentence.

| flies | right | why | high | first |
|-------|-------|------|------|-------|
| breath | slide | clouds | lies | frosty |

7. When people _____ saw penguins, they thought

they were fish.

8. It is easy to see _____ they made that mistake.

9. Penguins are birds that do not soar in the _____.

10. Instead, a penguin "_____" in the water.

11. It jumps _____ every few feet.

12. A penguin does this so it can take a _____ of air.

13. Penguins can leap up on the cold, _____ land.

14. To move on land, a penguin sometimes _____
down on its belly.

15. It can then scoot and _____ quickly on the ice.

16. Penguins have just the _____ bodies for their
habitats.

Name _____  Date _____

# Regular Plurals

**Focus**

To make many words plural, meaning "more than one," add the ending -s or -es. These types of plurals are called **regular plurals,** because they follow these rules.

- The letters -es are added to words ending in *ch, sh, s, ss, x, z,* or *zz.*

  box + es = boxes

- If a word ends in a *consonant* + *-y,* change the *y* to *i,* and add -es.

  fly + es = flies

- If a word ends in a *vowel* + *-y,* just add -s.

  toy + s = toys

- If a word ends in *f* or *fe,* change the *f* or *fe* to *v,* and add -es.

  knife – fe + ves = knives

**Practice**  Circle the correct spelling for each word. Write the correct spelling on the line.

**1.** pillowes    pillows    _____

**2.** berrys    berries    _____

**3.** cowboys    cowboies    _____

**4.** foxs    foxes    _____

**5.** porches    porchies    _____

**6.** elephants    elephantes    _____

**Apply**  Think about how to make each word from the box plural. Sort the plural word into the correct group.

| desk | mess | horse | baby | wish |
|------|------|-------|------|------|
| fly | wolf | donkey | life | slide |

Group 1: Add -es

**7.** _____

**8.** _____

Group 2: Add -s

**9.** _____

**10.** _____

**11.** _____

**12.** _____

Group 3: Change *y* to *i* and added -es

**13.** _____

**14.** _____

Group 4: Change *f* or *fe* to *v* and add -es

**15.** _____

**16.** _____

Name _____ Date _____

# Selection Vocabulary

**Focus**

**except** (ek•sept')
*prep.* only (page 140)

**maze** (māz) *n.* a confusing
series of paths or
passageways through
which people might get lost
(page 142)

**bacteria** (bak•tēr'•ē•ə) *n.*
plural form of **bacterium:**
a tiny living cell that can
be seen only through a
microscope. Some cause
disease; others help, such as
making soil richer (page 146)

**hollow** (hol'•lō) *adj.* having a
hole or an empty space inside
(page 146)

**stored** (stord) *v.* a form of the
verb **store:** to put away for
future use (page 147)

**dwellers** (dwel'•ûrz) *n.* plural
form of **dweller:** a person
or an animal that lives in a
certain place (page 150)

**swarming** (sworm'•ing) *adj.*
moving in a large group
(page 152)

**Practice**    **Match each vocabulary word with its clue.**

1. maze

2. dwellers

3. swarming

4. hollow

5. stored

a. a puzzling path

b. the going of a group

c. the center of a cave

d. a squirrel's hidden snack

e. hamsters in their home

**Apply** The underlined vocabulary words have gotten mixed up. Cross out each word, and write the correct word beneath each sentence.

6. <u>Hollow</u> help to make good soil called humus.

   _____

7. You could buy humus at a garden store, <u>swarming</u>—you can make it!

   _____

8. You can put plant waste in the <u>dwellers</u> of a bin.

   _____

9. Bacteria come <u>except</u> to this waste.

   _____

10. These trash <u>hollow</u> live there and change garbage into good soil.

    _____

11. Many people help plants by using humus they <u>bacteria</u>.

    _____

12. I once went through a <u>dwellers</u> made out of a corn field.

    _____

Name _____ Date _____

# Writing a Summary

**Think**  **Audience: Who** will read your summary?

_____

**Purpose: What** is your reason for writing the summary?

_____

**Prewriting**  **Use this graphic organizer to take notes for your summary.**

☐ Write the main idea of the article or book you are summarizing in the *Topic* box.

☐ Put other important ideas, such as examples, reasons, and facts, in the *Subtopic* boxes.

☐ Write the conclusion of the article or book in the *Conclusion* box.

| Topic |
|---|
|  |

| Subtopic | Subtopic |
|---|---|
|  |  |

| Conclusion |
|---|
|  |

## Revising — Use this checklist to revise your summary.

- ☐ Is the main idea stated in the first sentence?
- ☐ Take out any information you did not get from the article or book.
- ☐ Did you use time and order words? Will they help readers follow the order of events?
- ☐ Does your writing sound serious and informative?

## Editing/Proofreading — Use this checklist to correct mistakes.

- ☐ Did you indent your paragraph?
- ☐ Did you use correct spelling?
- ☐ Did you capitalize the title of the book or article?
- ☐ Is the book title underlined, or is the article title put in quotation marks?
- ☐ Did you end each sentence with correct punctuation?

## Publishing — Use this checklist to prepare your summary for publication.

- ☐ Neatly rewrite or type a final copy.
- ☐ Make a cover for your summary.

Name _____ Date _____

# Spelling

**Focus** To make most words **plural,** add -s or -es. For words that end in:

- *ch, sh, s, ss, x, z,* or *zz,* add -es.
- consonant + -*y,* change the *y* to *i* and add -es.
- *f,* change the *f* to *v,* and add -es.
- vowel + -*y,* just add an -s.
- silent -*e,* just add an -s.

/ī/ can be spelled *igh, _y,* and *_ie.*

**Practice** Sort the spelling words under the correct heading.

**Added -s**

1. _____

**Ends in *ch*, added -es**

2. _____

**Changed -*y* to *i*, added -es**

3. _____

4. _____

5. _____

### Word List

1. *lie*
2. *ties*
3. *fly*
4. *flies*
5. *halves*
6. *cycles*
7. *reply*
8. *replies*
9. *sigh*
10. *monkeys*
11. *lunches*
12. *fight*
13. *knights*
14. *spy*
15. *spies*

### Challenge Words

16. *dwellers*
17. *outcry*

**/ī/ spelled _y**

6. _____

7. _____

8. _____

**Singular words /ī/ spelled _igh_ and -_ie_**

9. _____

10. _____

11. _____

**Vowel -_y_, added -_s_**

12. _____

**Silent _e_, added -_s_**

13. _____

14. _____

**_f_ to _v_, added -_es_**

15. _____

**Name** _____ **Date** _____

# Possessive Nouns and Pronouns

**Focus**

A **possessive noun** shows ownership.

To make a possessive out of

- a single noun, add -'s.

  girl   +   's   =   girl's

- a plural noun ending in s, add just an apostrophe (').

  boys +   '   =   boys'

- a plural noun <u>not</u> ending in s, add -'s.

  children   +   's   =   children's

A **possessive pronoun** also shows ownership. It takes the place of a possessive noun. Some possessive pronouns are *my, our, your,* and *its.*

the girl's house ⟶ her house

**Practice**

**Rewrite each group of words using a possessive noun or pronoun.**

**1.** the car belonging to Jerry _____

**2.** the tail of the elephant _____

**3.** the food of the children _____

**4.** the laces on the shoes _____

**5.** the book that belongs to her _____

**Apply** Rewrite each sentence using a possessive pronoun.

**6.** Abdul saw the family's house.

_____

**7.** The mother cat's paw was sore.

_____

**8.** The men's cars were nearby.

_____

**The writer of this summary paragraph made some mistakes. Cross out the incorrect possessives. Write the correct words in the margin.**

In her story "A Possum Guide," Lizzy Rust tells how a thing changed her life. One day, Rust was in her's garden. She felt sad. Suddenly, she found a tiny baby possum. A possum is a small furry animal. She wanted it to be her pet. She called a shelter, which is a place that helps sick animals. The shelters owner said Rust had to give it to them. Rust kept thinking about that baby animal. Finally, she knew what she needed to do. She learned how to take care of animals. Rusts's new job is helping animals like that possum.

Name _____ Date _____

# Note-Taking Guidelines

**Note taking is an important part of investigation.**

- After finding information in a book or magazine, it is important to write notes about the information.

- Note taking gives you a chance to look at your information later and review it in order to learn it and remember it.

**Guidelines for Taking Notes**

- Use a different page for each kind of information that you collect.

- Create a heading for each kind of information.

- Write most of your notes in your own words. Do not just copy down the author's words. Write key phrases, and use abbreviations. Summarize what you have learned.

- If you want to use the author's exact words, place them in quotation marks. Also include the author's name, the book title, and the page number of the quotation.

- Write down only the most important facts and ideas about your research question or problem.

- Write neatly.

**Apply**  Use the library or the Internet to find information about Chicago, Illinois. Take notes on the information you find. You may wish to research one of the following topics:

**Grant Park**      **Lake Michigan**      **Chicago River**

**Topic:** _____

**Heading:** _____

**Notes:** _____

_____

_____

_____

**Heading:** _____

**Notes:** _____

_____

_____

_____

**Heading:** _____

**Notes:** _____

_____

_____

_____

Name _____ Date _____

# /ō/ Sound/Spellings

- /ō/ can be spelled *oa* at the beginning or in the middle of words. Example: <u>oa</u>t, m<u>oa</u>t
- /ō/ can also be spelled _*ow* at the end of words. Example: r<u>ow</u>

**Practice** A word is missing in each sentence. Choose the word with /ō/ to complete each sentence. Write the word on the blank line.

**1.** The _____ grew straight and tall.
(owk  oak)

**2.** I could not move fast, so I was _____.
(slowe  slow)

**3.** Quinn _____ out on the lake.
(rowed  roed)

**4.** The man could not lift the heavy _____.
(load  loed)

**5.** High winds pushed the small _____.
(bowt  boat)

**6.** Penelope was _____ the grass.
(mowing  moaing)

**Apply**  Part of a word containing /ō/ is missing in each sentence below. Read the clue about the missing word. Write the missing letters to complete the word.

7. There is a Vietnamese story about a _____ oa _____.

   (Clue: a small green animal)

8. In the story, there had been no rain or _____ _____ ow for years.

   (Clue: frozen white water)

9. The toad and a group of animals walked the _____ oa _____ to the Sky King's home.

   (Clue: a kind of path)

10. All he saw was a toad, so Sky King sent Thunder to

    _____ _____ ow it away.

    (Clue: what the wind does)

11. But all the animals fought Thunder; they made Sky King

    _____ _____ ow tired.

    (Clue: what a plant does when it gets taller)

12. Sky King said, "I give up. Now whenever toad grinds his teeth,

    I'll make rain _____ _____ ow again.

    (Clue: what a river does)

Name _____ Date _____

# Irregular Plurals

**Focus** Some plurals do not follow the regular pattern.
- Some words, such as *deer* and *shrimp,* have the same singular and plural forms.
- Some words, such as *goose* and *geese,* change spellings in the plural form.     Example: *tooth, teeth*     *man, men*

**Practice** Sort each word from the box under the correct heading.

| | | |
|---|---|---|
| teeth | fish | oxen |
| geese | mice | sheep |

**Words with the same singular and plural.**

1. _____     2. _____

**Words with spelling changes**

3. _____     5. _____

4. _____     6. _____

**Apply**  Make each noun plural. Write it on the line.
(Remember: Some words have the same singular
and plural forms.)

**7.** one deer     several     _____

**8.** one child     many     _____

**9.** one moose     three     _____

**10.** one shrimp     a bucket of     _____

**11.** one goose     a flock of     _____

**12.** one tooth     thirty-two     _____

**13.** one person     many     _____

**14.** one foot     two     _____

**15.** one man     two     _____

**16.** one cactus     many     _____

Name _____ Date _____

# Selection Vocabulary

**Focus**

**strange** (strānj) *adj.* unusual (page 163)

**enormous** (ē•nor'•məs) *adj.* very big (page 163)

**hatch** (hach) *v.* to come out of an egg (page 164)

**responsibility** (ri•spon'•sə•bi' •li•tē) *n.* a duty (page 166)

**bringing up** (bring'•ing•up) *n.* raising, as in children (page 166)

**beckoned** (bek'•ənd) *v.* past tense of **beckon:** to call someone by waving (page 168)

**Practice** Circle the word in parentheses that best fits each sentence.

**1.** In "The Ugly Duckling," a duck found a (strange/hatch) egg in her nest.

**2.** When the chick (beckoned/hatched), the duck thought he was ugly.

**3.** Because he was her (responsibility/enormous), the duck took care of him.

**4.** Other ducks and animals made fun of the (enormous/beckoned) bird.

**5.** But when the grown-up animal saw some swans, they (hatch/beckoned) to him.

**6.** They showed him that the mother duck had actually been (beckoned/bringing up) a beautiful swan.

**Apply**    **Read each sentence. Answer each question by explaining the definition in your own words.**

**7.** Annika <u>beckoned</u> to her friend.

Describe what Annika did.

_____

**8.** Setting the table is my <u>responsibility</u>.

Why do I set the table?

_____

**9.** The baby alligator <u>hatched</u>.

What did the baby alligator do?

_____

**10.** Paulo thought the color was <u>strange</u>.

What did Paulo think about the color?

_____

**11.** The sisters pretended that they were <u>bringing up</u> their dolls.

What did the sisters pretend to do?

_____

**12.** Aiden could not finish the cookie because it was <u>enormous</u>.

Why could Aiden not finish the cookie?

_____

**Name** _____ **Date** _____

# Fantasy and Reality

**Focus** An author may write a story that is based on reality or on fantasy.

- **Fantasy** stories are stories that could not happen in real life. A fantasy story may have make-believe characters, such as genies or fairies.

- A story based on **reality** is realistic. It tells of something that could happen in real life.

**Practice** Read the list of story topics. Write an *F* beside each topic that is a fantasy story. Write an *R* beside a topic that is realistic.

**1.** Ali, Juan, and Sue go to school. _____

**2.** A cat speaks in poems. _____

**3.** A giant eats the trees in your backyard. _____

**4.** A girl's family moves to a new town. _____

**5.** A boy breaks a window with a football. _____

**6.** Three girls fly out of their bedroom windows at night. _____

**7.** Cali's pig can fly around his farm. _____

**8.** Kevin gets a toy truck for his birthday. _____

**Apply** **Read the following paragraph. Answer the questions about the story described.**

In the book *Strega Nona,* a woman named Strega Nona has a pot with special powers. If she says certain words, it will make pasta. One day Strega Nona leaves Big Anthony in charge of her house. He wants to make pasta. He says the words, and the pot makes pasta. But he cannot make it stop. Strega Nona comes home just before the pasta takes over the town. To teach him a lesson, she makes Big Anthony eat all that pasta.

**9.** Do you think this is a fantasy story or a realistic story?

_____

**10.** Give two examples to support your answer.

_____

**11.** Explain how these examples are fantasy or reality.

_____

**Choose one of the realistic story topics from the Practice section on the previous page. Write the topic below. Then, write ideas of how to turn it into a fantasy story.**

**12.** Topic chosen:

_____

How would you turn it into a fantasy story?

_____

**Name** _____ **Date** _____

# Choosing an Investigation Question

**Use this page to write down questions that you or your group have about animals and animal habitats. Think of questions that may be fun, interesting, and useful to investigate.**

**Question 1:** _____

_____

Why would this question be helpful or interesting to research?

_____

_____

**Question 2:** _____

_____

Why would this question be helpful or interesting to research?

_____

_____

**Question 3:** _____

_____

Why would this question be helpful or interesting to research?

_____

_____

**Use this page to narrow down your possible investigation questions. Choose one question to investigate with your group.**

Write the question here: _____

_____

A good investigation will help you learn new things. How will investigating this question be useful or helpful to your group, the class, and others? What do you expect to learn?

_____

_____

_____

_____

One question may lead to many other questions about your topic. List some of your new investigation questions.

_____

_____

_____

_____

Name _____ Date _____

# Writing a Nonfiction Book Review

**Think**

**Audience: Who** will read your book review?

_____

**Purpose: What** is your reason for writing the book review?

_____

**Prewriting** Use this outline to take and arrange notes for your book review.

(Book title)　　**I.** _____

(Main idea)　　**A.** _____

(Supporting details)

　　　　　　　　　**1.** _____

　　　　　　　　　**2.** _____

　　　　　　　　　**3.** _____

(Opinion)　　　**B.** _____

(Details to Support Opinion)

　　　　　　　　　**1.** _____

　　　　　　　　　**2.** _____

## Revising — Use this checklist to revise your book review.

☐ Do you use reasons and details to support your opinion?

☐ Do you tell the plot's main idea in the first sentence?

☐ Do you follow the order of events?

☐ Does your review sound as though you liked or disliked the book?

## Editing/Proofreading — Use this checklist to correct mistakes.

☐ Did you indent your paragraphs?

☐ Did you use correct spelling?

☐ Did you capitalize the title of your book or article?

☐ Is the book title underlined?

☐ Did you use correct punctuation for quotations?

## Publishing — Use this checklist to prepare your book review for publication.

☐ Neatly rewrite or type a final copy.

☐ Add a drawing or computer graphic.

Name _____ Date _____

# Spelling

**Focus** **Irregular plurals** are words that do not add -s or -es to the base word to form a plural.

Some words have the same singular and plural form. *deer*

Some words change spelling altogether. *goose, geese*

/ō/ can be spelled _ow and oa.

**Practice** **Sort the spelling words under the correct heading.**

**Plural words spelled the same as the singular**

1. _____

2. _____

**Plural words that change spelling**

3. _____

4. _____

5. _____

6. _____

## Word List

1. *low*
2. *mice*
3. *women*
4. *coach*
5. *deer*
6. *throw*
7. *roast*
8. *teeth*
9. *crow*
10. *oxen*
11. *bow*
12. *loan*
13. *grow*
14. *float*
15. *fish*

## Challenge Words

16. *cacti*
17. *pillow*

**/ō/ spelled _ow**

7. _____

8. _____

9. _____

10. _____

11. _____

**/ō/ spelled _oa_**

12. _____

13. _____

14. _____

15. _____

Name _____ Date _____

# Plural Nouns and Irregular Plural Nouns

**Focus** Nouns name a person, place, thing, or idea.

| Rule | Example |
|---|---|
| • Most regular nouns form the plural by adding -s to singular nouns. | • The **carpenters** cut boards for the house. |
| • For regular nouns ending with s, ch, sh, ss, z, zz, or x, add -es to singular nouns. | • These **bushes** need to be cut down. |
| • For regular nouns ending with a consonant and y, change the y to i and add -es. | • The **babies** slept all afternoon. |
| • Some nouns are irregular when they form the plural and do not follow these rules. Check a dictionary for the spelling. | • The **mice** ran around while the **oxen** stayed in the barn. |

**Practice** Circle the regular plural nouns.

The Chen family likes to go to amusement parks. The children love to ride on the Ferris wheels, glide down the water slides, and drive the bumper cars. They play games with toys for prizes. Last year, Ming was tall enough to ride the roller coasters.

**Apply** Circle the correct plural from each pair.

Jamie, Victor, and I never thought we would see a family of **deer deers** the night we camped out in my backyard. We were in the tent eating **blueberries blueberrys** and playing **games gamies** using our **flashlights flashlightes.** The lights were as bright as **torchs torches**. Suddenly, **shadowes shadows** loomed up on the tent. Victor whispered, "I bet they are **sheep sheeps**!" We crept out of the tent as quiet as **mouses mice**. The **deers deer** stood there as still as **statues statueis**.

**Delete each boldface noun and write its plural above it.**

Every spring we go to my aunt's house to have a

family dinner. When we enter, she smothers the **child**

with **kiss.** All the family members come to eat. There

are so many people that we eat two **turkey** and three

pies. After dinner, the **man** watch football, the women

talk in the kitchen, and the **baby** sleep. I look forward

to this each year because I get to see all my cousins

from Georgia and my two **uncle** who moved to Rome,

Italy. When we leave, my mom always says, "We have

enough leftovers to make **lunch** for a week!"

**Name** _____ **Date** _____

# Tables and Charts

Information can sometimes be presented in charts or tables. Charts and tables show a lot of information in a small amount of space. Information is listed in columns and rows to help you easily and quickly find specific information.

| Favorite Wildlife in Our Neighborhood | | | | |
|---|---|---|---|---|
| **Class** | **Tree** | **Insect** | **Animal** | **Wildflower** |
| Grade 1 | white oak | ant | raccoon | goldenrod |
| Grade 2 | maple | praying mantis | squirrel | violet |
| Grade 3 | live oak | caterpillar | hawk | purple aster |
| Grade 4 | blue spruce | praying mantis | raccoon | milkweed |
| Grade 5 | sycamore | honeybee | mouse | violet |

**Using the chart above, answer the following questions.**

**1.** What is the title of the chart?

_____

**2.** What classes gave information for the chart?

_____

**3.** What is Grade 3's favorite animal? _____

# Natural Habitats and City Habitats Chart

As you read about and investigate city wildlife, record here what you find out about city animals' natural habitats and what they find familiar in the city.

| Animal | Natural Habitat | What makes it feel at home in the city? |
|--------|-----------------|------------------------------------------|
|        |                 |                                          |
|        |                 |                                          |
|        |                 |                                          |
|        |                 |                                          |

Study Skills • *Skills Practice 1*

Name _____ Date _____

# /ū/ Sound/Spellings

**Focus**

- /ū/ can be spelled _ew at the end of a word. Example: *few*

- /ū/ can be spelled _ue at the end of a word. Example: *cue*

**Practice** Read each word below. Circle any letters that spell /ū/. Cross out the word if no letters spell that sound.

1. pew

2. untie

3. rescue

4. hew

5. skew

6. barbecue

7. flow

8. curfew

9. nephew

10. crust

**Apply** Read each pair of words below. Circle the correct spelling.

**11.** mue        mew

**12.** argue        arguew

**13.** view        viuew

**14.** value        valew

**Read the rough draft of the paragraph below. Cross out the four spelling errors. Write the correct spellings above the crossed-out words.**

How to Pack for a Backpacking Trip

First, lay out your backpack. Check your tent and

sleeping bag for rips. Make a list of what you would

like to take. Bring things such as food, water, extra

clothes, a flashlight, and an emergency kit. Bring a

camera to capture the voo. Continew gathering things.

Try to pack your bag. Weigh it. Is your backpack too

heavy? Revoo your list. You may have to take a fuew

things out to make your backpack lighter. Once your

bag is packed, you are ready to go.

Name _____ Date _____

# Homographs

**Homographs** are words that have the same spelling, but have different pronunciations and meanings.
Example: *Live* and *live* are homographs.
 *live* (liv)   "to make one's home"
 *live* (līv)   "live animals at the zoo"
You can learn the meanings of homographs and how to pronounce them. Then, when you read one in a sentence, you will understand which word is being used.

**Read the following sentence, and answer the questions about it.**

Robin Hood shot an arrow from his bow.

**1.** Do the letters *ow* in *bow* make the /ow/ sound from *now* or the /ō/

sound as in *know?* _____

**2.** What is the meaning of the word *bow* in the sentence?

_____

**3.** Say *bow* with the /ow/ sound. The words *bow* (bow) and *bow* (bō) are homographs. Find the definitions for the two words in a dictionary.

*bow* (bow) _____

*bow* (bō) _____

**Apply**  **Answer each question below.**

**4.** The words *dove* and *dove* are homographs. Notice that they have the same spelling. What is the meaning of the word *dove* in the context of the following sentence?

The young <u>dove</u> had white feathers.

dove: _____

**5.** Circle how the word *dove* is pronounced in the sentence above.

duv    dōv

**6.** What is the meaning of the word *dove* in the context of the sentence below?

The swimmer *dove* into the cold water.

dove: _____

**7.** Circle how the word *dove* is pronounced in the sentence above.

duv    dōv

**8.** Write your own sentence using the word *dove*.

_____

_____

Name _____ Date _____

# Selection Vocabulary

**Focus**

**male** (māl) *adj.* of or having to do with men or boys (page 178)

**female** (fē'•māl) *n.* a woman or girl (page 178)

**aboard** (ə•bord') *adv.* on or into a ship, train, or airplane (page 181)

**mainland** (mān'•lənd) *n.* the chief landmass of a country, or continent, as different from an island (page 181)

**mild** (mīld) *adj.* gentle or calm; not harsh or sharp (page 182)

**layer** (lā'•ûr) *n.* one thickness of something (page 182)

**population** (pop'•ū•lā'•shən) *n.* the number of people or animals who live in a place (page 182)

**balance** (bal'•əns) *n.* a steady, secure position (page 189)

**Practice** Circle the correct vocabulary word to complete each sentence below.

**1.** A doe is a (male/female) deer.

**2.** Saul tripped because he lost his (aboard/balance).

**3.** There is a (mainland/population) of rabbits living in the woods.

**4.** A (mild/female) wind ruffled the leaves.

**5.** When it is cold outside, you should wear many (layers/populations).

**Apply**   **Poems sometimes have pairs of lines that end in rhyming words. Write the vocabulary word that rhymes with each underlined word or words.**

**6.** There once was a duck—a strong _____

Who tried swimming, but always would <u>fail</u>.

**7.** So from all of the duck _____

He would ask for good swim <u>information</u>.

**8.** But although the duck had many <u>talents</u>,

In the water he fell and lost _____.

**9.** Until once as he sat on the _____

He saw a boat come toward that <u>same land</u>.

**10.** With great joy, he jumped up and ran <u>toward</u>,

Asking, "Please, now—could I come _____?"

**11.** Up he climbed; there he stood like the <u>mayor</u>

Of the sea's many parts and each _____.

**12.** "I will sail now—no swimming!" He <u>smiled</u>.

And he rode off on seas soft and _____.

Name _____ Date _____

# Making Inferences

**Focus**

Readers get ideas, or **make inferences,** about characters or events in a story. They use information the writer gives them and add it to what they already know to make a new idea.

Example: "Paul heard a long whistle in the distance. He knew his father would arrive soon."

- You know that trains whistle and that people sometimes travel on them.

- You make an inference that Paul's father is coming on a train.

**Practice** **Read the following background information and sentences. Then, answer the question below.**

In this part of *Peter Pan,* Peter had lost his shadow. He has just found it, but the shadow will not stick to him.

He tried to stick it on with soap from the bathroom, but that also failed. A shudder passed through Peter, and he sat on the floor and cried. (from *Peter Pan* by J. M. Barrie)

**1.** What does the writer tell you in these sentences?

_____

**2.** Based on what you know, why do people cry?

_____

**3.** Why is Peter crying? What inference can you make?

_____

**Apply** **Read this paragraph. Draw a line under the inference you can make. Use the information in the paragraph and what you already know.**

**4.** The three boys worked hard for their father. The oldest cleaned up the shop every day and helped his father make clothes. The middle son also helped by cleaning up and making clothes. The youngest son helped by delivering the finished clothes to the customers. He tried his best to work on the clothes, too.

**Inference:**

The father has three daughters.

The father is a baker with his own bakery.

The father makes clothes in his own shop.

**5. Read the following paragraph. Answer the question.**

The fog over the ocean was thick and heavy. From the deck, Sharon caught a glimpse of a bright, flashing light, however, and knew they were close to the shore. She was eager to see her family at the dock.

What inference can you make about what Sharon is riding on? Explain your answer.

_____

_____

_____

Name _____ Date _____

# Identifying Investigation Needs and Making Plans

Use these pages to make a plan to research the topic that you have chosen for your group investigation.

**Research Question:** _____

**List what you already know about your topic:** _____

_____

_____

_____

**What do you think you might discover about your investigation topic?** Remember that finding more information will help you confirm or revise your conjectures.

_____

_____

**What questions do you still need to investigate?** _____

_____

_____

_____

**Create a list of people who may be experts about your topic.**

_____

_____

# Identifying Investigation Needs and Making Plans (continued)

There are several kinds of sources of information. In your group, decide which of the sources below will be useful. Check whether you think each source would be useful or not useful.

| Possible Sources | Useful | Not useful |
|---|---|---|
| Encyclopedias | | |
| Books | | |
| Magazines | | |
| Newspapers | | |
| Films or TV shows | | |
| Interviews | | |
| Personal Observation | | |
| Museums | | |
| Internet sites | | |
| Others | | |

For each useful source that you checked, write down a specific title, person, or place you could use as a possible source for information. Then, write how each source could be useful.

Title or Name of Source: _____

How this source will be useful: _____

_____

Title or Name of Source: _____

How this source will be useful: _____

_____

Name _____ Date _____

# Explaining a Process

**Think**  **Audience: Who** will read your explanation?

_____

**Purpose: What** is your reason for explaining this process?

_____

**Prewriting**  Use this graphic organizer to prepare to explain a process. Write the steps of your process in the boxes in order.

**Chain of Events**

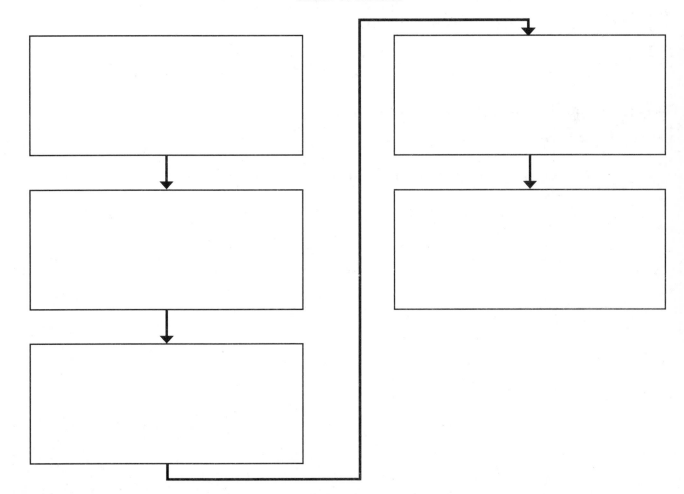

## Revising

**Use this checklist to revise your explanation of a process.**

☐ Did you include all the necessary steps?

☐ Are the sentences in the best order to help readers understand the process?

☐ Are your words clear and specific?

☐ Is your writing easy to understand?

## Editing/Proofreading

**Use this checklist to correct mistakes.**

☐ Did you use correct spelling?

☐ Did you use correct punctuation?

☐ Did you capitalize the title of your explanation?

☐ Are words such as *First, Next,* and *Finally* in order?

## Publishing

**Use this checklist to prepare for publication.**

☐ Neatly rewrite or type a final copy.

☐ Make a chart to show the steps in your process.

**Name** _____  **Date** _____

# Spelling

**Focus** **Homographs** are words that have the same spelling, but have different pronunciations and meanings.

/ū/ can be spelled _ew and _ue.

**Practice** Sort the spelling words under the correct heading.

**Homographs**

1. _____

2. _____

3. _____

4. _____

5. _____

6. _____

7. _____

**/ū/ spelled _ew**

8. _____

9. _____

10. _____

**Word List**

1. cue
2. few
3. well
4. rose
5. argue
6. tire
7. hue
8. ring
9. value
10. change
11. spew
12. rescue
13. park
14. view
15. light

**Challenge Words**

16. pitcher
17. nephew

**/ū/ spelled _ue**

11. _____

12. _____

13. _____

14. _____

15. _____

Name _____ Date _____

# Types of Sentences

**Focus**

A **sentence** is a group of words that makes a complete thought about something. The first letter of the first word of a sentence is capitalized.

| Rule | Example |
|---|---|
| • **Declarative sentences** provide information. They end with a period. | • People who are different from each other can be friends. |
| • **Interrogative sentences** ask questions. They end with a question mark. | • When will my letter arrive? |
| • **Exclamatory sentences** show strong emotion. They end with an exclamation point. | • I wish my friend's letter would arrive! |
| • **Imperative sentences** give commands or make requests. They end with a period. | • Give me that letter. |

**Practice** Identify each sentence as declarative, exclamatory, interrogative, or imperative.

**1.** I really want to go on a trip! _____

**2.** When will we leave? _____

**3.** We'll fish for our dinner. _____

**4.** Take me down the Mississippi River. _____

**Apply** **Finish each sentence with the correct punctuation.**

**5.** Do you want to go with us _____

**6.** Yes, I want to go _____

**7.** Wow, look at that plane _____

**8.** Watch out _____

**Read the draft of Danny's letter below. Help him edit his letter. Underline three times letters that should be capitals. Insert the correct end punctuation.**

Dear Joey,

How are you we learned something really interesting today in school It was about baseball we learned that a man named Jackie Robinson was the first African American to play in the Major Leagues Many white people did not want him to play. They called him names and made threats against him why did they treat him that way It doesn't make sense to me he was a great ballplayer Why wouldn't they want a player who would help them win He didn't let anyone get in his way He became a star for the Dodgers he was very brave

Your friend,
Danny

Name _____  Date _____

# Diagrams

**Focus**  A **diagram** is a plan, drawing, or outline that shows how something works, that labels or explains parts of something, or that shows the relationship between parts of something.

**Practice**  **Look at the diagram of THE TONGUE. Use the diagram to answer the questions.**

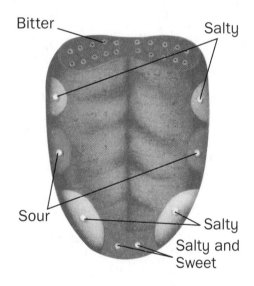

1. What taste bud is at the back of the tongue? _____

2. What taste buds are on the tip of the tongue?

   _____

3. What taste buds are on the sides of the tongue?

   _____

**Apply**

**Look at the diagram of THE EAR. Use the diagram to answer the questions.**

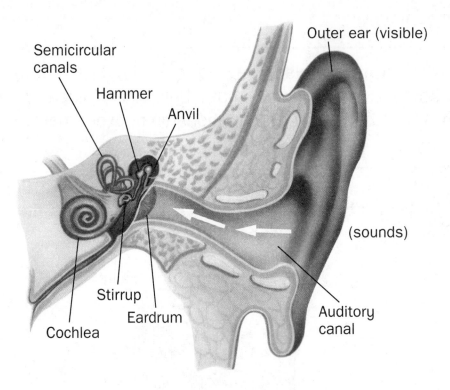

4. Name the part of the ear that you can see.

_____

5. Through what part of the ear do noises enter?

_____

6. What part of the ear is farthest from the outer ear?

_____

Name _____ Date _____

# /ī/, /ō/, /ū/ Sound/Spellings, and Consonant Blends

**Focus** Remember the following sound/spellings.

- /ī/ can be spelled *igh* at the end or in the middle of words or *_ie* at the end of a word.

Example: *si**gh**, t**ie***

- /ō/ can be spelled *oa* at the beginning or in the middle of words or *_ow* at the end of words.

Example: *__oa__t, r__ow__*

- /ū/ can be spelled *_ew* or *_ue* at the end of a word. Example: *f__ew__, c__ue__*

- Remember: **Consonant blends** are strings of consonants in which you can hear each letter's sound. They are usually at the beginning or end of words. Example: *__tr__uck, __spl__ash*

**Practice** **Write *Yes* if the word has a long vowel sound or a consonant blend. Circle the letters that spell the sound or blend. Write *No* if the word has neither.**

**1.** thighs _____

**2.** loud _____

**3.** argue _____

**4.** soap _____

**5.** lash _____

**6.** bedroom _____

**Apply**   **Write a word from the box to complete each sentence.**

| trapped | argued | throats | stalked | rescued |
|---|---|---|---|---|
| moonlight | frightened | value | snowy | roam |

**7.** For many years, wolves scared and _____ people.

**8.** Wolves often _____ and harmed farm animals.

**9.** So most wolves in this country were _____ and killed.

**10.** But people _____ against this choice.

**11.** They said wolves were important and had

_____.

**12.** Now, in some parks, wolves again run and

_____.

**13.** This plan has _____ wolves.

**14.** Now, you might see a wolf on a park's white,

_____ hills.

**15.** You can hear howls from wolves' _____ again.

**16.** You can see their dark shapes in the _____.

Name _____ Date _____

# Homophones

**Focus**
**Homophones** are words that sound alike but have different spellings and different meanings. Think about the meaning of the word when deciding how to spell a homophone correctly.

Example: *Sea* and *see* are homophones.

The words sound alike:     sea (sē)          see (sē)

But they have different meanings:

   *sea* "a large body of saltwater"

   *see* "to look at with the eyes"

**Practice**    **Read the sentence. Then, answer the questions below.**

Anne pointed and said, "Put the book <u>here</u>."

**1.** What is the meaning of *here* in the sentence?

_____

**2.** The words *here* and *hear* are homophones. What do the two words have

in common? _____

**3.** What is the meaning of *hear?* _____

**4.** Use *hear* or *here* to complete this sentence:

   The boys _____ the bells ringing.

**Apply** **Answer each question below.**

5. What is the meaning of the underlined word in the sentence below?

   The bird's feathers were <u>blue</u>.

   _____

6. What is the meaning of the underlined word in the sentence below?

   The wind <u>blew</u> the bird's feathers.

   _____

7. The words *blue* and *blew* are homophones. Explain how you know

   they are homophones.

   _____

8. What is the meaning of the underlined word in the sentence below?

   She drew a <u>new</u> picture.

   _____

9. What is the meaning of the underlined word in the sentence below?

   She <u>knew</u> her mother would like the picture.

   _____

10. Are *new* and *knew* homophones? Why or why not?

   _____

Name _____ Date _____

# Selection Vocabulary

**Focus**

**relocates** (rē•lo'•kāts) *v.* a form of the verb **relocate:** to move to a new place (page 204)

**stranded** (strand'•əd) *v.* a form of the verb **strand:** to leave in a helpless position (page 204)

**exclaimed** (eks•klāmd') *v.* past tense of **exclaim:** to speak out (page 205)

**sharp** (shärp) *adj.* alert (page 205)

**detect** (də•tekt') *v.* to find out (page 205)

**cautiously** (kosh'•əs•lē') *adv.* with close care (page 205)

**appreciate** (əp•prē'•shē•āt') *v.* to understand the value of (page 205)

**extended** (eks•tend'•əd) *v.* past tense of **extend:** to reach out (page 210)

**Practice** Circle the correct word to complete each sentence.

1. Li's family (relocated/exclaimed) to a new town, and today she started school.

2. She walked down the hallway (detect/cautiously).

3. Li tried to seem brave, but she felt lost and (extended/stranded).

4. "Hi—are you new?" a voice (relocated/exclaimed).

5. Li turned, and a girl (extended/exclaimed) her hand with a smile.

6. Li somehow knew this girl would (appreciate/sharp) her worries.

**Apply** Read each clue. Write the correct vocabulary word in the boxes. When you have written all the words, write each circled letter in the matching numbered blank to answer the riddle below.

7.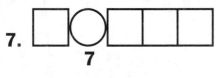

paying attention

8.

to notice

9.

moves to a new place

10.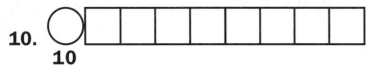

said loudly

11.

left alone

12. **Why wouldn't the zoo animals let the big cat play games with them?**

He was a ___ ___ ___ ___ ___ ___ ___ .
9 7 10 10 8 11 7

Name _____  Date _____

# Collecting Information for Inquiry

**Use these pages to record new information that you gather for your group's research investigation. List your sources, any new information, and any new questions about your topic below.**

**Title or name of source:** _____

New information about your topic: _____

_____

_____

Does any information in this source change your ideas about your topic

at all? How? _____

_____

New questions that you need to answer: _____

_____

**Title or name of source:** _____

New information about your topic: _____

_____

_____

Does any information in this source change your ideas about your topic

at all? How? _____

_____

New questions that you need to answer: _____

_____

**Title or name of source:** _____

New information about your topic: _____

_____

_____

Does any information in this source change your ideas about your topic

at all? How? _____

_____

New questions that you need to answer: _____

_____

**Title or name of source:** _____

New information about your topic: _____

_____

_____

Does any information in this source change your ideas about your topic

at all? How? _____

_____

New questions that you need to answer: _____

_____

Name _____ Date _____

# Writing a Realistic Story

**Audience: Who** will read your realistic story?

_____

**Purpose: What** is your reason for writing this realistic story?

_____

**Prewriting**

**Use this graphic organizer to prepare to explain a process.**

**Story Map**

| Beginning: |
|---|
| |

↓

| Middle: |
|---|
| |

↓

| End: |
|---|
| |

## Revising

**Use this checklist to revise your realistic story.**

☐ Could your characters, setting, and events be real?

☐ Will your beginning interest the reader?

☐ Is there a problem to be solved?

☐ Does your order of events make sense?

☐ Did you use dialogue?

☐ Is the problem solved?

## Editing/Proofreading

**Use this checklist to correct mistakes.**

☐ Did you use correct spelling?

☐ Did you use correct punctuation?

☐ Did you use quotation marks around dialogue?

☐ Is it clear who is speaking when you use dialogue?

## Publishing

**Use this checklist to prepare your realistic story for publication.**

☐ Neatly rewrite or type a final copy.

☐ Give your story a title.

**Name** _____ **Date** _____

# Spelling

**Focus** **Homophones** are words that sound alike but have different spellings and different meanings.

Notice words with:

/ī/ spelled *igh*, *_y*, and *_ie*

/ō/ spelled *_ow* and *oa*

/ā/ spelled *a_e*

Remember that **consonant blends** are groups of two or three letters in which the sound of each letter can be heard.

**Practice** **Sort the spelling words under the correct heading.**

**Group homophones into pairs**

1. _____  _____

2. _____  _____

3. _____  _____

4. _____  _____

5. _____  _____

6. _____  _____

7. _____  _____

**Word List**

1. groan
2. grown
3. seam
4. seem
5. piece
6. peace
7. by
8. buy
9. toe
10. tow
11. horse
12. hoarse
13. meet
14. meat
15. tale

**Challenge Words**

16. waste
17. waist

**/ā/ spelled *a_e***

8. _____

Name _____ Date _____

# Replacement Pronouns, and Nouns as Subject and Object

**Focus**

Remember that a **subject** is whom or what a sentence is about. A **direct object** receives the action of the verb.

| Rule | Example |
|---|---|
| • A noun can be the **subject** of a sentence. | • The <u>dog</u> ate. |
| • A noun can also be the **direct object** of a sentence. | • The dog ate the <u>food</u>. |
| • A **pronoun** can replace the object noun in a sentence. | • The dog ate <u>it</u>. (<u>It</u> replaces the object noun <u>food</u>.) |

**Practice**

Draw a line under the subject noun or nouns in each sentence. Circle the direct object noun.

**1.** Beatrix Potter wrote many children's books.

**2.** Potter lived an interesting life.

**3.** Potter kept several pets while growing up.

**4.** Her family took trips to a place called the Lake District.

**5.** Potter and her brother loved animals.

**Apply**  Read each pair of sentences. Cross out the direct object noun in the second sentence. Replace it with the correct pronoun.

**6.** Potter had many pets. Potter drew

her pets and became a very good artist.

**7.** Potter wrote stories. She wrote stories

about rabbits, ducks, and lots of other animals.

**8.** When she was fifteen, Potter began keeping a secret

journal. She wrote her journal using a secret code.

**9.** *The Tale of Peter Rabbit* is one of Potter's most famous stories.

She wrote *The Tale of Peter Rabbit* about her pet rabbit, Peter.

**The writer of this paragraph made two mistakes when replacing direct object nouns with pronouns. Cross out each incorrect pronoun. Write the correct pronoun.**

England's Lake District is well known for being the

home of Beatrix Potter. Beatrix Potter loved him. Once

she was married, Potter ran her own farm in the District.

She had some special sheep. These sheep were

disappearing. Potter helped save her. Potter helped

found the National Trust. This group worked to protect

the land. When she died, she left thousands of acres of

land to the Trust. She helped save the land she loved.

Name _____ Date _____

# Graphic Organizers

**Look at the different types of graphic organizers.**

### Details Web

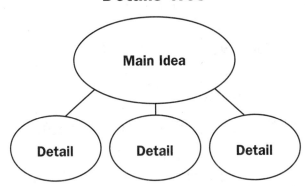

### Time Line

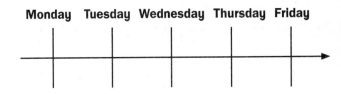

### Chain of Events

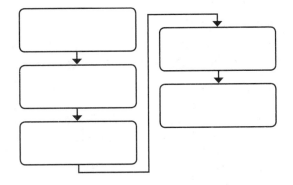

### Character Web

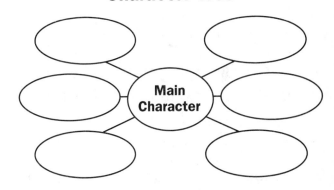

### Descriptive Detail

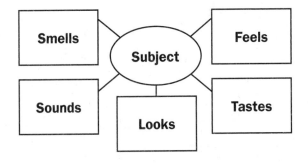

### Venn Diagram

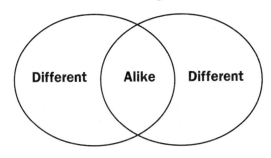

## Graphic Organizers (continued)

**Choose the graphic organizer from the previous page that would be the best organizer to use for each problem below.**

**1.** Jordan wants to write a story about one week at school. Make sure he tells what happened in order. _____

**2.** Toni is writing a story about a talking horse named Sam. Make sure she has good character descriptions. _____

**3.** Brianna is writing a story about going to the circus. She wants her readers to experience the circus like she did. _____

**4.** Michael wants to write a comparison of his old house in Ohio and his new house in Colorado. He needs to make sure he writes about how they are alike, as well as how they are different. _____

**5.** Marcus is writing a news story about the football game. He needs to make sure he has all of his facts in the correct order.

_____

**6.** Elizabeth is trying to persuade her school to recycle. She needs to make sure she gives good reasons. _____

Name _____ Date _____

# /o͞o/, /ū/ Sound/Spellings and Open and Closed Syllables

- /o͞o/ can be spelled *oo* in the middle and at the end of a word. Example: sh<u>oo</u>t

- /o͞o/ can be spelled _ue at the end of a word. Example: cl<u>ue</u>

- /o͞o/ can be spelled _ew at the end of a word. Example: n<u>ew</u>

- /o͞o/ can be spelled u_e at the end of a word. Example: fl<u>ute</u>

- Remember that /ū/ shares _ew and _ue spellings with the /o͞o/ sound. Example: f<u>ew</u>, c<u>ue</u>

- An **open syllable** ends in a vowel. The vowel sound is usually long. Example: spī·der

- A **closed syllable** ends in a consonant. The vowel sound is usually short. Example: r<u>ab</u>·b<u>it</u>

**Practice**  **Use slashes to divide the following words into syllables. Circle open syllables. Draw a line under closed syllables.**

**1.** napkin

**2.** object

**3.** unit

**4.** moment

**5.** item

**6.** menu

**7.** unless

**8.** program

**Apply**  Write the correct spelling to complete each sentence below.

9. Some Native Americans tell a story about the first

(floot/flute). _____

10. In it, a young man (groo/grew) to love a woman.

_____

11. An old man told him to make a flute from a

(loose/luse) branch. _____

12. The young man found the branch, and (scuped/scooped)
and carved the wood.

_____

13. Then the old man told him to wait for the next

(mune/moon). _____

14. The man followed his (rules/rooles) and waited.

_____

15. When he played, the soft breeze gave him ideas

for his (tune/toone). _____

16. The woman heard him, and her heart (groo/grew)

light. _____

17. "I (choose/chews) you," she said. _____

18. Because of the first flute, they found (troo/true)

love. _____

Name _____  Date _____

# Review of Regular and Irregular Plurals, Homographs, and Homophones

**Focus**

| Plurals | Example |
|---|---|
| • For many plurals, add -*s* or -*es*. If a word ends in a *consonant* + -*y,* change the *y* to *i,* and add -*es*. | • *bench**es**, toys, fl**ies*** |
| • Some plurals do not follow this pattern. | • *goose, g**ee**se; deer, deer* |
| **Homographs** are words that are <u>spelled</u> alike, but have different pronunciations and meanings. | • *read* (rēd), *read* (red) |
| **Homophones** are words that <u>sound</u> alike, but have different spellings and meanings. | • *see* (sē), *sea* (sē) |

**Practice**  **Label each pair of underlined words *homographs* or *homophones*.**

**1.** The squirrel filled the <u>hole</u> in the tree with <u>whole</u> acorns.

**a.** homographs   **b.** homophones

**2.** The white <u>dove</u> <u>dove</u> out of the sky.

**a.** homographs   **b.** homophones

**3.** Judah could not <u>hear</u> the music <u>here.</u>

**a.** homographs     **b.** homophones

**4.** People used to <u>record</u> music on a <u>record</u>.

**a.** homographs     **b.** homophones

**5.** The man <u>read</u> the <u>red</u> book.

**a.** homographs     **b.** homophones

**Apply**    **Write the plural form of each word below.**

**6.** box    _____

**7.** man    _____

**8.** train    _____

**9.** berry    _____

**10.** mouse    _____

**The writer of this paragraph made four mistakes spelling plurals and homophones. Cross out each mistake, and write the correct spelling.**

     John Muir studied plants and animals. He lived

in California. Muir spent a lot of time hiking and

camping. He traveled over mountaines and through

forests. He saw deers and other animals. He worked

to right books about these things. Muir's writinges

helped get our country to create many parks.

Name _____  Date _____

# Selection Vocabulary

**Focus**

**habitats** (hab'•it•ats') *n.* plural form of **habitat:** the place where an animal or plant naturally lives and grows (page 220)

**rich** (rich) *adj.* able to produce much; fertile (page 227)

**variety** (vər•ī'•ə•tē') *n.* a number of different things (page 228)

**patch** (pach) *n.* a small area (page 229)

**migrating** (mī'•grāt'•ing) *adj.* moving from one place to another (page 233)

**vast** (vast) *adj.* very great in size (page 234)

**prey** (prā) *n.* an animal that is hunted by another animal for food (page 236)

**recognize** (rek'•əg•nīz') *v.* to know and remember from before; to identify (page 239)

**Practice**    Read each sentence. Think about the meaning of the underlined word. Decide if the sentence is *True* or *False*.

**1.** A lion is a zebra's prey.

  **True**    **False**

**2.** A whale's habitat is the ocean.

  **True**    **False**

**3.** The Rocky Mountains are vast.

  **True**    **False**

**4.** When a bear sleeps through the winter, it is migrating.

  **True**    **False**

**5.** A baby duck knows its mother because it recognizes her.

  **True**    **False**

**1.** Keisha and her dad hiked in a very wide, _____ canyon.

**2.** Parts of the dry canyon were _____ for desert lizards and coyote.

**3.** But along the river, many plants grew in the _____, wet soil.

**4.** Keisha's dad could _____ and tell her about many plants.

**5.** They saw monarch butterflies _____ to the warm canyon from the north.

**6.** Birds do not like them as their _____ because monarchs taste bad.

**7.** Keisha saw a desert rat on a small _____ of ground.

**8.** They saw a great _____ of plants and animals.

Name _____ Date _____

# Classify and Categorize

**Focus** Sometimes when you learn new ideas, it is helpful to place them into a group, or category. A **category** is the title for a group of things. When you put ideas into groups, you are **classifying and categorizing.**

Example: Category: Types of Flowers

Items to Classify: daisy, rose, daffodil, lilac

**Practice** Think about the words in the box below. Then, answer the questions underneath it.

| | | | |
|---|---|---|---|
| bricks | cement | silk | clay |
| cotton | wood | stone | wool |

1. Circle the category that <u>all</u> the words fit into.

   **a.** Things People Should Eat

   **b.** Materials to Make Things With

   **c.** Materials Used to Make Clothes

   **d.** Things That Grow

2. **What two groups could be made from the group?**

   _____

**Apply** Classify each word from the box on the previous page in the Practice section. Write it under the correct category.

| Materials Used to Make Houses | Materials Used to Make Clothes |
| --- | --- |
|  |  |
|  |  |
|  |  |
|  |  |
|  |  |

Suppose you and your family are going on vacation. Think of one category of things you will need to pack and take with you. Write down the things from that category.

Category: _____

Items: _____

_____

_____

Name _____  Date _____

# Writing an Informative Report: Rough Draft

**Think** | **Audience: Who** will read your report?

_____

**Purpose: What** is your reason for writing this report?

_____

**Prewriting** | Use this graphic organizer to prepare to write a rough draft of your report.

**Expository Structure**

| Topic: |
| --- |

| Subtopic: | Subtopic: |
| --- | --- |
|  |  |

| Conclusion: |
| --- |

## Revising
**Use this checklist to revise your rough draft.**

- ☐ Do you have a strong beginning?
- ☐ Are your ideas in the best order?
- ☐ Did you stick to your topic?
- ☐ Did you sum up your ideas in the conclusion?

## Editing/Proofreading
**Use this checklist to correct mistakes.**

- ☐ Did you use correct spelling?
- ☐ Did you use correct punctuation?
- ☐ Did you use quotation marks around dialogue?
- ☐ Are the names of people and places capitalized?

## Publishing
**Use this checklist to prepare your report for publication.**

- ☐ Write or type a neat final copy.
- ☐ Save it to use when making your finished report.

**Name** _____ **Date** _____

# Spelling

**Focus** /ōō/ can be spelled oo, _ew, u_e, _ue, and u.

**Word List**

1. clue
2. tuna
3. root
4. June
5. flute
6. blue
7. chew
8. choose
9. glue
10. noodle
11. truth
12. blew
13. stew
14. duty
15. rude

**Challenge Words**

16. jewel
17. duet

**Practice** Sort the spelling words under the correct heading.

**/ōō/ spelled oo**

1. _____

2. _____

3. _____

**/ōō/ spelled _ew**

4. _____

5. _____

6. _____

**/ōō/ spelled u_e**

7. _____

8. _____

9. _____

**/o͞o/ spelled _ue**

10. _____

11. _____

12. _____

**/o͞o/ spelled u**

13. _____

14. _____

15. _____

Spelling • *Skills Practice 1*

# Pronouns as Subject

Name _____ Date _____

**Focus**

Remember that the **subject** is what a sentence is about. A **pronoun** can take the place of a subject noun.

Example:

Subject Noun:       <u>Queen Elizabeth</u> ruled England.

Subject Pronoun:    <u>She</u> ruled England.

When replacing a noun with a pronoun, make sure you use a pronoun that shows the same number and gender.

Example:

Subject Noun:       The <u>boy</u> kicked the ball.

Subject Pronoun:    <u>She</u> kicked the ball.   → WRONG

                    <u>They</u> kicked the ball.  → WRONG

                    <u>He</u> kicked the ball.    → CORRECT

**Practice**   Circle each subject pronoun. Write *P* if it is plural and *S* if it is singular.

**1.** They rode on a bus. _____

**2.** She made her bed. _____

**3.** It rolled away. _____

**4.** He did not play the piano. _____

**5.** They grew tall in the sun. _____

 Read each pair of sentences. Write the subject pronoun that takes the place of the subject in the first sentence.

**6.** Theodor Geisel wrote many books for children.

_____ wrote them under the name *Dr. Seuss.*

**7.** His mother had the last name Seuss. _____ came to America from Germany.

**8.** Many publishers did not like his first book. _____ said his books did not teach and should not rhyme.

**9.** Dr. Seuss proved they were wrong. _____ wrote fun books about important ideas.

**10.** *The Lorax* is a book about pollution. _____ tells about a disappearing forest.

**11.** *The Sneetches* is a book about friendliness. _____ shows that how people look does not matter.

**12.** Now his books are very famous. _____ are still very popular.

Name _____ Date _____

# Indexing

This is a page from the index of a book called *Finding Out about Our Feathered Friends.* Use it to answer the questions on the next page.

Mourning dove. *See* Dove.

National Audubon Society, The, 3, 14, 79, 85

Nests

building, 31–42

cleaning, 43–45, 47

materials for, 32–35, 38, 50

sites for, 31–33, 36, 78, 100

*See also* individual birds.

Oriole, 15, 18

Osprey, 34, 48–49, 82

Owl

description, **51,** 90–93

mating, 25

nests, 35

*See also* Barn owl, Great horned owl.

Parakeet

and learning, 14–16

caring for, 15

Parrot

imitating human speech, 19–20

life span, 18

Passenger pigeon, 61–63, **87**

Pelican

description, 115

mating, 28

migration, 65

Pigeon

babies, 49–50

calls, 12

description, 61–63, **87**

in the city, 91–92

mating, 26

nests, 39

*See also* Dove, Passenger pigeon, Racing pigeon.

Quail, 80

Racing pigeon, **87,** 91

Raven, 13, 35, 81–82

**Apply**

**1.** How many topics are there that start with the

letter *O*? _____

What are they?

_____

**2.** On which pages can you find information about

*Parrots?* _____

**3.** What subtopics are listed under *Parakeet?*

_____

**4.** What specific types of owls does the index refer you

to under the topic *Owl?* _____

_____

**5.** Is there a listing in the index for *Raven?* _____

**6.** On which pages can you find information about

*Materials for Nests?* _____

**7.** On which page can you find a description of

a *Pelican?* _____

**8.** On which pages can you find information about the

*National Audubon Society?* _____

Name _____ Date _____

# The /ōo/ and /oo/ Sound/Spellings

Remember that /ōo/ can be spelled *oo* in the middle of a word. Examples: *m<u>oo</u>n, s<u>oo</u>n*

But *oo* can also spell **/oo/** in the middle of a word. Examples: *l<u>oo</u>k, w<u>oo</u>d*

**Practice** Write each word from the box in the correct group.

| hoofbeats | room | took | woolen |
|-----------|----------|--------|--------|
| football | booming | sooner | stood |

**The /ōo/ sound**

1. _____

2. _____

3. _____

**The /oo/ sound**

4. _____

5. _____

6. _____

7. _____

8. _____

**Apply**

Read the word in the box. Change the word in the box to make a new rhyming word that completes the sentence. Write the new word on the blank line.

9. | looking | Alejandro wanted to learn to cook, so he signed up

for _____ lessons.

10. | took | He bought a _____ with recipes to follow.

11. | wood | His teacher, Mrs. Crawford, gave him

_____ cooking tips.

12. | stood | She showed him that a spoon made of

_____ would not scratch nonstick pans.

13. | boom | She taught Alejandro to leave

_____ between each roll so they
can spread out.

14. | boo | He learned to bake rolls and

cook dinner _____.

15. | moon | _____ he was cooking all kinds of things.

16. | shook | Alejandro was glad he _____ the lessons.

Name _____    Date _____

# The Inflectional Ending -*ing*

**Focus**

The inflectional ending **-ing** means that the action is happening now or always happens. For words that end in short vowels and a consonant, double the final consonant before adding -*ing*.

$$clap \longrightarrow clapping$$

For words that end with a silent e, drop the e before adding -*ing*.

$$tape \longrightarrow taping$$

For words ending in a consonant or *y*, add -*ing*.

$$sail \longrightarrow sailing$$

$$study \longrightarrow studying$$

**Practice**    **Circle the correct spelling of each word. Write the correct spelling on the line.**

**1.** shining    shineing    _____

**2.** runing    running    _____

**3.** pasing    passing    _____

**4.** prizing    prizeing    _____

**5.** skiping    skipping    _____

**6.** biting    biteing    _____

**Apply**

**The writer of these sentences forgot to use *-ing*. Rewrite each underlined word correctly adding *-ing*.**

**7.** When Tyler was six he took <u>swim</u> lessons.

_____

**8.** He was nine years old when he started <u>skateboard</u>.

_____

**9.** He also learned ice-<u>skate</u>.

_____

**10.** His father spent time <u>build</u> him skate ramps and <u>drive</u> him to the ice rink.

_____        _____

**11.** Tyler enjoyed <u>make</u> new friends.

_____

**12.** He liked <u>win</u> prizes and trophies.

_____

**13.** People loved <u>watch</u> him ice-skate and skateboard.

_____

**14.** But then he started <u>like</u> other sports.

_____

**15.** So, he started <u>play</u> hockey and soccer.

_____

Name _____ Date _____

# Selection Vocabulary

**Focus**

**deal** (dēl) *n.* an agreement (page 258)

**ancient** (ān' • shənt) *adj.* very old (page 258)

**traders** (trā' • dûrz) *n.* plural form of **trader:** a person who buys and sells things as a business (page 259)

**valuable** (val' • ū • bəl') *adj.* worth much money (page 260)

**solution** (sə • lo͞o • shən) *n.* the answer to a problem (page 261)

**kingdom** (king' • dəm) *n.* a country that is ruled by a king or a queen (page 261)

**eventually** (ē • ven' • chə • lē) *adv.* finally (page 262)

**forms** (formz) *n.* plural form of **form:** kind; type (page 262)

**Practice**   Read each sentence. Write *Yes* if the definition matches the way the underlined word is used. Write *No* if it does not.

**1.** The "Silk Road" is the name of an <u>ancient</u> trading route.

**finally** _____

**2.** <u>Traders</u> took the Silk Road all the way from China to Egypt.

**people who buy and sell** _____

**3.** People in Rome loved wearing <u>valuable</u> silk clothes.

**costly** _____

**4.** Silk was made only in China, a <u>kingdom</u> far from Rome.

**answer to a problem** _____

**Apply** Use the clues to complete the crossword puzzle below.

## Across

**8.** worth much money

**12.** people who buy and sell things as a business

## Down

**5.** an agreement

**6.** the answer to a problem

**7.** finally

**9.** very old

**10.** a country ruled by a king or queen

**11.** kinds or types

Name _____ Date _____

# Generating Ideas and Questions

**List things here that you already know about money:**

_____

_____

_____

_____

**Given the things you know already know about money, list things that you still wonder about or want to know about money:**

_____

_____

_____

_____

_____

_____

_____

_____

**List things here that your group finds most interesting about money:**

_____

_____

_____

_____

**Good investigation questions usually begin with _how_ or _why_. Take each thing you found interesting about money and ask a question about it beginning with _how_ or _why_. These questions are potential questions to investigate:**

_____

_____

_____

_____

_____

_____

_____

_____

_____

Name _____ Date _____

# Timed Writing

**Think**  **Audience: Who** will read your writing on a timed test?

_____

**Purpose: What** is your reason for writing this composition?

_____

**Prewriting**  **Use these reminders as you write your timed composition.**

- Write about a special place you like to go.

- Explain what the special place is like.

- Explain why you like going there.

- Make sure your writing is interesting to the reader.

- Make sure each sentence you write helps the reader understand your composition.

- Make sure your ideas are clear and easy for the reader to follow.

- Write about your ideas in detail so that the reader understands what you are saying.

- Check your work for correct spelling, capitalization, punctuation, grammar, and sentence structure.

## Revising

**Use this checklist to revise your composition.**

☐ Did you underline each thing you were asked to write about in the reminders?

☐ Did you make notes before writing?

☐ Did you respond to each reminder?

## Editing/Proofreading

**Use this checklist to correct mistakes.**

☐ Did you indent your paragraphs?

☐ Did you use correct spellings?

☐ Did you capitalize the first word of each sentence?

☐ Did you end each sentence with correct punctuation?

Name _____ Date _____

# Spelling

**Focus**   When adding the inflectional ending **-ing,** for words with a silent e, drop the e before adding -ing. For words with a short vowel-consonant pattern, double the final consonant before adding -ing.

**/oo/** is spelled oo and makes the sound as in the word foot.

**Practice**   **Sort the spelling words under the correct heading.**

-ing added to words with silent e

1. _____

2. _____

3. _____

-ing added to words with short-vowel consonant patterns

4. _____

5. _____

-ing added

6. _____

7. _____

8. _____

**Word List**

1. took
2. wood
3. landing
4. brook
5. playing
6. timing
7. hood
8. batting
9. amazing
10. stood
11. good
12. hopping
13. hoping
14. shook
15. meaning

**Challenge Words**

16. woodwork
17. staring

/oo/ spelled *oo*

9. _____

10. _____

11. _____

12. _____

13. _____

14. _____

15. _____

Name _____ Date _____

# Sentence Structure

**Focus**

| Rule | Example |
|---|---|
| • A **simple sentence** has one subject and one predicate. | • **The United States** is over two hundred years old. |
| • A **compound sentence** uses a conjunction to combine two simple sentences. Use the conjunctions *and*, *but*, and *so* to join simple sentences that relate to each other. Place a comma before the conjunctions. | • The United States is a country, **and** France is a country.<br>• Miami is in the United States, **but** Paris is in France.<br>• It is warm in Miami, **so** I wanted to work there. |

**Practice** After each sentence, write **S** if the sentence is simple or **C** if it is compound.

**1.** California and Florida are states. _____

**2.** California is on the West Coast, but Florida is on

the East Coast. _____

**3.** California's capital is Sacramento, and Florida's

capital is Tallahassee. _____

**4.** Florida is also called the Sunshine State. _____

**Practice** **Underline the compound sentences.**

Kathi Littlejohn is a Cherokee storyteller. She learns the tribal legends from her elders. The Cherokee legends teach the history of their people, and they encourage people to treat one another with respect. Littlejohn knows many of the Cherokee legends, but most people do not know them. She tells the stories for other people to learn.

**Add commas before the conjunctions in the compound sentences.**

The Polynesian peoples sang chants to commemorate important events in life. Many chants were about birth and other chants were about love, death, or war. Some chants commemorated the birth of a child but some chants commemorated smaller events such as losing a tooth. The people dressed flamboyantly for some chants and they dressed simply for others. They chanted alone or in groups. Sometimes the men chanted alone but many times the men and women chanted together.

Name _____ Date _____

# Time Lines

> **Focus** A **time line** is a graph that shows when things happen over time.
>
> - Each dot on a time line stands for a date or time.
> - Each dot stands for a single event.
> - Events are listed from left to right in the order they happened. The earliest event is at the far left.

**Practice** Use the time line to answer the questions below.

### Early Life of the Wright Brothers

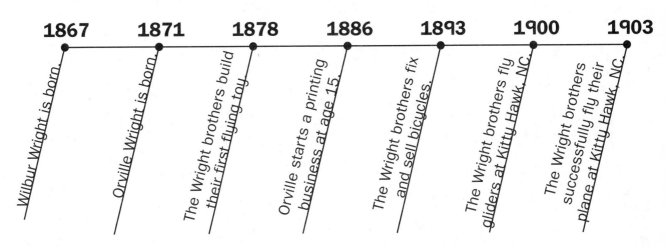

| 1867 | 1871 | 1878 | 1886 | 1893 | 1900 | 1903 |

Wilbur Wright is born.

Orville Wright is born.

The Wright brothers build their first flying toy.

Orville starts a printing business at age 15.

The Wright brothers fix and sell bicycles.

The Wright brothers fly gliders at Kitty Hawk, NC.

The Wright brothers successfully fly their plane at Kitty Hawk, NC.

**1.** What is the subject of this time line?

_____

**2.** When did Orville start a printing business?_____

**3.** Which event happened first: Wilbur Wright is born or Orville Wright is born? _____

**4.** What happened in 1895? _____

**Apply**  **Imagine your class is going on a field trip to the zoo. What might you do while you are there? Write five ideas on the lines below.**

**5.** _____

**6.** _____

**7.** _____

**8.** _____

**9.** _____

**The trip will begin at 9:00 A.M. and end at 12:00 P.M. Decide what time each of your events will happen. Write your events in order on the time line below.**

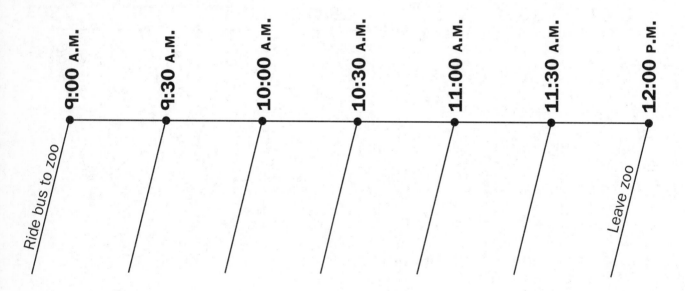

Name _____ Date _____

# The /ō/ and /ow/ Sound/Spellings

**Focus**
- /ō/ can be spelled _ow at the end of words. Examples: kn*ow*, sh*ow*
- /ow/ is often spelled *ou*. /ow/ is sometimes spelled *ow* at the end or near the end of a word. Examples: s*ou*nd, n*ow*

**Practice** Write a word from the box that rhymes with each underlined word to complete a line of each poem.

| know | gown | frown |
|------|------|-------|
| grow | row | brown |

**1.** Isabelle, Isabelle, runs around <u>town</u>,

Isabelle, Isabelle, in a pink _____.

What is the trouble? Oh, why do you _____?

Isabelle is a big bear that is _____!

**2.** Out in my garden there's something to <u>show</u>.

It's rather unusual, I want you to _____.

For sprouting up in it, all lined in a _____,

Trees made of chocolate have started to _____.

**Read each sentence below. Circle the correct spelling.**

3. There is a fable about a (crou/crow).

4. This bird was flying (around/arownd) and became thirsty.

5. She (fownd/found) a pitcher of water.

6. But when she tried to drink, the water was too (loa/low).

7. The bird could not change the (amount/amownt) of water.

8. Instead, she looked on the (grownd/ground) near the pitcher.

9. There were (thowsands/thousands) of tiny pebbles.

10. The bird picked up pebbles and dropped them (doun/down) in the water.

11. Each pebble made the water rise, and soon the bird could reach the water with her (mouth/mowth).

12. That bird was smart, without a (doubt/dowt)!

Name _____ Date _____

# The Inflectional Ending -ed

**Focus**

Adding **-ed** to a verb makes the action *past tense,* or something that happened in the past.

- For words that end in /a/, /e/, /i/, /o/, or /u/ and a consonant, double the final consonant before adding *-ed.*

    tap $\longrightarrow$ ta**pp**ed

- For words that end with a silent e, drop the e before adding *-ed.*

    carve $\longrightarrow$ carv**ed**

- For words ending in consonant *-y,* change the y to i before adding *-ed.*

    study $\longrightarrow$ stud**ied**

**Practice**

**Read each sentence. Write *Yes* if *-ed* was used correctly. Write *No* if it was not.**

1. Christopher Columbus <u>sailed</u> to new places. _____

2. The Spanish king and queen <u>wantted</u> him to go. _____

3. He <u>traveld</u> with three ships in August. _____

4. They <u>landed</u> on an island in October. _____

5. Columbus thought it was Asia and <u>nameed</u> it "the Indies." _____

6. The crew <u>looked</u> for gold on nearby islands. _____

7. On the way home, one ship <u>wrecked</u>. _____

**Apply** Rewrite each sentence, changing the underlined verb to the verb with *-ed*.

**8.** I <u>open</u> the door. _____

**9.** We <u>hike</u> the trail. _____

**10.** Randy and Karen <u>enter</u> the room. _____

**11.** I <u>blink</u> my eyes. _____

**Read the sentences below. The writer made four mistakes when adding *-ed*. Cross out each mistake, and write the correct spelling.**

Hayley and her mother went door-to-door in their

neighborhood selling cashews and trail mix to raise

money for a school trip. She hopeed that someone would

buy some.

"What are you selling?" her neighbor, Mr. Pickles, asked.

"Cashews and trail mix," Hayley replyed.

Mr. Pickles pulled out his wallet. "I'll buy one of each,"

he said.

Hayley smiled and thankked him.

Mr. Pickles seemmed happy as Hayley walked away.

Name _____ Date _____

# Selection Vocabulary

**Focus**

**seal** (sēl) *n.* an official stamp (page 272)

**portrait** (por' • trət) *n.* a picture of someone (page 274)

**debts** (dets) *n.* plural form of **debt:** something that is owed to another (page 276)

**formula** (for' • mū • lə') *n.* a set method for doing something (page 280)

**counterfeit** (koun' • tûr • fit') *adj.* fake (page 280)

**emblem** (em' • bləm) *n.* a sign or figure that stands for something (page 285)

**remains** (rē • mānz') *v.* a form of the verb **remain:** to be left (page 287)

**inspect** (in • spekt') *v.* to look at closely (page 287)

**Practice** Match each vocabulary word with its example.

**1.** remains

**2.** portrait

**3.** counterfeit

**4.** inspect

**5.** formula

**6.** debts

**7.** emblem

**8.** seal

**a.** look at

**b.** bills to be paid

**c.** is left behind

**d.** a painting of George Washington

**e.** the symbol of a college

**f.** a king's stamp

**g.** directions for making tea

**h.** a fake coin

**Apply** Write the vocabulary word that completes each sentence.

9. Fake or _____ dollar bills have always been a problem.

10. People who make them cannot use the real

_____ for making money.

11. Instead, they copy George Washington's

_____ on the bill.

12. They fake the Great _____, or stamp, of the United States.

13. The figures on this _____ show the ideas of peace and strength.

14. People sometimes use fake money to pay

off _____.

15. The money then _____ in use and takes value from real money.

16. You can help stop this crime by learning how to

_____ your dollar bills.

**Name** _____ **Date** _____

# Sequence

**Focus**

**Sequence** is the order in which events take place in a text. Sequence can be expressed with time or order words.

- Words that tell when things happen are called **time** words. They include *today, earlier, before, after,* and *yesterday.*

- Words that tell the order in which things happen are called **order** words. They include *first, second, next, last, then,* and *finally.*

**Practice** **Look through "The Go-Around Dollar" for examples of story events that happen in a certain order. Write examples of story events in the correct order, using time or order words to show the correct sequence of events.**

**1.** Page: _____ Events in order: _____

_____

_____

Time or order words: _____

**2.** Page: _____ Events in order: _____

_____

_____

Time or order words: _____

**Practice** Read the sentences and underline the time or order word or words in each sentence.

**3.** Wednesday we will go to the park before we eat dinner.

**4.** Last week I did all my homework plus some extra-credit work.

**5.** Next month is my birthday.

**6.** I was born after my sister.

**7.** Babies learn to crawl before they can walk.

**Apply** Read the following sentences and use them to write a paragraph. Use time or order words to place events in a clear sequence.

We stopped for fruit smoothies on the way home.

We rented bicycles.

We went to the park with Mom.

We biked on a park trail through the woods.

_____

_____

_____

_____

_____

Name _____ Date _____

# Choosing an Investigation Question

**Use this page to write down questions about money your group thinks would be fun, interesting, or useful to investigate.**

**Question 1:** _____

_____

Why would this question be helpful or interesting to research?

_____

_____

**Question 2:** _____

_____

Why would this question be helpful or interesting to research?

_____

_____

**Question 3:** _____

_____

Why would this question be helpful or interesting to research?

_____

_____

## Choosing an Investigation Question (continued)

Use this page to narrow down the questions on the previous page to one question your group wants to investigate.

The question that our group finds most interesting or most useful to research is:

_____

_____

A good investigation will help people learn new things. How will investigating this question be useful or helpful to your group, the class, and others?

_____

_____

_____

_____

One question may lead to many questions that you would like to find out about. These are some other questions related to our question or topic:

_____

_____

_____

_____

Inquiry · *Skills Practice 1*

Name _____ Date _____

# Writing a Summary

**Think**  **Audience: Who** will read your summary?

_____

_____

**Purpose: What** is your reason for writing the summary?

_____

_____

**Prewriting**  **Use this graphic organizer to take notes for your summary.**

☐ Write the main idea of the article or book you are summarizing in the *Topic* box.

☐ Put other important ideas, such as examples, reasons, and facts, in the *Subtopic* boxes.

☐ Write the conclusion of the article or book in the *Conclusion* box.

| Topic |
| --- |
| |

| Subtopic #1 | Subtopic #2 |
| --- | --- |
| | |

| Conclusion |
| --- |
| |

## Revising    Use this checklist to revise your summary.

- ☐ Is the main idea stated in the first sentence?
- ☐ Take out any information you did not get from the article or book.
- ☐ Did you use time and order words? Will they help readers understand your summary?
- ☐ Does your writing sound serious and informative?

## Editing/Proofreading    Use this checklist to correct mistakes.

- ☐ Did you indent your paragraph?
- ☐ Did you use correct spellings?
- ☐ Did you capitalize the title of your book or article?
- ☐ Is the book title underlined, or is the article title put in quotation marks?
- ☐ Did you end each sentence with correct punctuation?

## Publishing    Use this checklist to prepare your summary for publication.

- ☐ Neatly rewrite or type a final copy.
- ☐ Make a cover for your summary.

Name _____ Date _____

# Spelling

**Focus** When adding the inflectional ending **-ed,** for words with a silent e, drop the e before adding -ed. For words with a short vowel-consonant pattern, double the final consonant before adding -ed. For words ending in consonant -y, change the y to i before adding -ed.

**/ow/** is spelled ou_ and ow as in the word cow.

**Practice** **Sort the spelling words under the correct heading.**

-ed added to words with silent e

1. _____

2. _____

3. _____

-ed added to words with short-vowel consonant patterns

4. _____

5. _____

-ed added to words ending in consonant -y

6. _____

7. _____

**Word List**

1. browse
2. shower
3. howl
4. couch
5. stripped
6. striped
7. married
8. jammed
9. named
10. tried
11. bored
12. noun
13. loud
14. mouse
15. crowd

**Challenge Words**

16. fountain
17. admitted

/ow/ spelled ou_

8. _____

9. _____

10. _____

11. _____

/ow/ spelled ow

12. _____

13. _____

14. _____

15. _____

Name _____ Date _____

# Comparative and Superlative Adjectives

**Focus**

An **adjective** describes a noun or pronoun. It tells what kind, how many, or which one. An adjective can tell how something feels or looks.

Example: Katie held the <u>tiny</u> frog. The frog was <u>green</u>.

**Comparative adjectives** compare two nouns.

- Add *-er* to most short adjectives to make them comparative.
- Use the word *more* before some longer adjectives.

Example: Kate's snake was <u>smoother</u> than the frog. Her bird is <u>more colorful</u> than the snake.

**Superlative adjectives** compare three or more nouns.

- Add *-est* to most short adjectives to make them superlative.
- Use the word *most* before some longer adjectives.

Example: The second frog is smaller than the first frog. The third frog is the <u>smallest</u> and the <u>most special</u> frog of all.

**Practice**

Read each sentence. If it has a comparative adjective, write *C* on the line. If it has a superlative adjective, write *S.*

**1.** The ocean is bigger than a lake. _____

**2.** That was the most terrible storm I have ever seen. _____

**3.** Kai was the tallest child in the class. _____

**4.** The baby's eyes were bluer than her mother's. _____

**Apply**
**Read each sentence. Rewrite the sentence and add one adjective.**

**5.** Jacob went into a store.

_____

**6.** Toys filled the shelves.

_____

**7.** Jacob bought a yo-yo.

_____

**8.** He looked at a bike.

_____

**Read the paragraph below. The writer made four mistakes using comparative and superlative adjectives. Correct each mistake.**

What is the tallest building? The answer keeps

changing. Someone will build a tall building. Then

someone else builds a more taller one. In 1913, the

Woolworth Building was the tallest. Then, the Empire

State building was built. It was more massiver. It was

the tallest for forty-one years. Next, the World Trade

Center appeared. Two years later, people built the Sears

Tower. Several years ago a building in Taiwan became

the taller in the world. It probably will not be tall for very

long, though!

Name _____ Date _____

# Using a Dictionary

**Practice**

**Look up the following words from "The Go-Around Dollar" in the Glossary and in a dictionary. Write the guide words from each source.**

1. emblem

   Glossary: _____ _____

   Dictionary: _____ _____

2. inspect

   Glossary: _____ _____

   Dictionary: _____ _____

3. portrait

   Glossary: _____ _____

   Dictionary: _____ _____

**Apply** Read the following dictionary entries. Circle the correct answer to each question below.

**lint** (lint) *n.* **1.** Clinging bits of fuzz. **2.** Fibers that cover cotton seed.

**4.** What is the entry word?

    **a.** *n.*                **b.** lint

**5.** Which word rhymes with the entry word?

    **a.** hint             **b.** bunt

**6.** Circle the number of the definition that matches this sentence:
The machine took the <u>lint</u> off the cotton.

    **a.** 1                **b.** 2

**villain** (vil' ən) *n.* **1.** A wicked or evil person. **2.** A character in a story or drama that fights against the hero.

**7.** What is the entry word?

    **a.** villain        **b.** (vil' ən)

**8.** Would this word come before or after the word *vote* in a dictionary?

    **a.** before        **b.** after

**9.** Circle the number of the definition that matches this sentence:
The <u>villain</u> in the play wore a black cape.

    **a.** 1                **b.** 2

Name _____ Date _____

# The /aw/ Sound/Spellings

**Focus**
The /**aw**/ sound can be spelled many ways.

/aw/ can be spelled:

- *aw* as in *raw*.
- *au* as in *sauce*.
- *augh* or *ough* in the middle of words. *caught, bought*
- *al* at the beginning or in the middle of words or *all* at the end of words. *almost, all*

**Practice**
**Circle each correct spelling. Write it on the line.**

**1.** daun     dawn     _____

**2.** taught     tought     _____

**3.** walk     wawk     _____

**4.** straugh     straw     _____

**5.** fawt     fought     _____

**6.** wall     wawl     _____

 Write the word from the box that completes each sentence.

| | | | | |
|---|---|---|---|---|
| talk | lawn | caught | crawled | tall |
| bought | called | walked | beanstalk | |

**7.** Once a boy named Jack _____
to town to sell his mother's cow.

**8.** A man _____ the cow for five
special beans.

**9.** Jack's mother was angry and threw the beans

on the _____.

**10.** But one bean grew into a very

_____ plant.

**11.** Jack climbed the _____ into
the clouds.

**12.** He went to an ogre's castle and

_____ into the oven to hide.

**13.** The ogre wanted to eat Jack, but Jack did not get

_____.

**14.** Jack took coins, a goose that laid golden eggs,

and a harp that could _____.

**15.** The harp _____ out, and the
ogre chased Jack.

Phonics • *Skills Practice 1*

# Regular Comparative and Superlative Adjectives

**Focus**

- Remember that **comparative adjectives** compare two nouns. Add *-er* to most short adjectives to make them comparative. Use the word *more* before some longer adjectives.

- **Superlative adjectives** compare three or more nouns. Add *-est* to most short adjectives to make them superlative. Use the word *most* before some longer adjectives.

- The castle was <u>taller</u> than Paul's house.
  The castle was <u>more wonderful</u> than Paul's house.

- That was the <u>smallest</u> butterfly I've ever seen.
  That was the <u>most colorful</u> butterfly I've ever seen.

**Practice** Decide whether the comparative adjective in each sentence should have *-er* or *more* added to it. Circle the correct choice.

1. The little boat was (faster/more fast) than the big boat.

2. The lake was (smoother/more smooth) this morning than yesterday afternoon.

3. The big boat was (expensiver/more expensive) than the small boat.

4. Today the wind felt (colder/more cold) than usual.

**Apply** Choose the correct superlative adjective for each sentence below.

5. That was the (wonderfulest/most wonderful) meal I've ever eaten.

6. The beans were the (greenest/most green) I've seen.

7. The store's tomatoes are sweet, my garden's tomatoes are sweeter, but these are the (sweetest/most sweet) tomatoes.

**Read each group of sentences. Use the information to write one sentence comparing the two objects. Use a comparative or superlative adjective in each sentence.**

8. This bed is six feet long. The crib is only four feet long.

_____

9. Steve is talking. Dave is shouting. Eric screams making the most noise.

_____

10. This book weighs five pounds. The other book weighs one pound.

_____

11. The kitchen is dark, but there is some light. There is no light in the basement.

_____

12. Tawana can lift twenty pounds. The other girls in gym class can each lift ten pounds.

_____

Name _____ Date _____

# Selection Vocabulary

**Focus**

**stack** (stak) *n.* a pile (page 301)

**profit** (prof' • it) *n.* the amount of money left after all the costs of running a business have been paid (page 303)

**expenses** (eks • pens' • əz) *n.* plural form of **expense:** money spent to buy or do something; cost (page 303)

**demand** (də • mand') *n.* the desire for a product or service (page 305)

**balance** (bal' • əns) *n.* to make equal in weight, amount, or force (page 306)

**supply** (səp • plī') *n.* a quantity of something ready to be used (page 306)

**product** (prod' • uct) *n.* anything that is made or created (page 306)

**competition** (kom' • pət • ish' • ən) *n.* the act of trying to win or gain something from another or others (page 307)

**Practice** Circle the correct vocabulary word that completes each sentence.

**1.** Eduardo and Maria had a big (stack/demand) of things to get rid of.

**2.** They decided to have a garage sale and try to make a (expenses/profit).

**3.** Their only (expenses/product) were the costs of making signs and flyers.

**4.** Maria said, "Let's have a (competition/product) to see who can sell the most stuff."

**5.** It was tricky to (profit/balance) selling items and giving people change.

**Apply**  **Read each pair of sentences. Write the vocabulary word that completes the second sentence.**

**6.** The potter made a cup to sell. The potter made

a _____.

**7.** Soccer teams from around the world tried to win the

World Cup. They had a _____.

**8.** After the store owner paid her bills, she had $1000

left over. The store owner had made a _____.

**9.** Yuri tried to organize his pile of papers. He had a big

_____ of papers.

**10.** Neela worked to make each pile of tomatoes the

same weight. She wanted to _____ them.

**11.** The theater had to spend money fixing broken seats.

The theater had _____.

**12.** On the first day of school, Harold had a big box of pencils.

Harold had a _____ of pencils.

**13.** Because of the hot day, beachgoers bought a lot of

ice water. There was a _____ for ice water.

Name _____ Date _____

# Fact and Opinion

**Focus** Writers often use facts and opinions to make their readers agree with them.

| Rule | Example |
|---|---|
| • A **fact** is a detail that is known to be true. Facts help readers believe what you write. They give information about your subject. They support your opinions. | • **Fact:** E. B. White wrote the books *Charlotte's Web* and *Stuart Little.* |
| • An **opinion** is what someone thinks or feels. Opinions cannot be proven true or false. You can use opinions and facts in the same piece of writing. Characters in stories can give opinions, too. | • **Opinion:** I think *Charlotte's Web* is a great book. |

**Practice** **Read each fact or opinion below. Explain why each is a fact or an opinion.**

**1.** Fact: Pierre is the capital of South Dakota.

_____

**2.** Fact: The Black Hills are in the western part of South Dakota.

_____

**3.** Opinion: I think the Black Hills are pretty.

_____

**Apply** Sometimes writers use facts to support their opinions. Draw a line between each opinion and a fact that supports it.

**Opinions**

4. The faces on Mount Rushmore are bigger than I thought they would be.

5. There are interesting things to see in the Black Hills.

6. Theodore Roosevelt was one of our best presidents.

7. Blasting a sculpture on a mountain sounds strange.

**Supporting Facts**

a. People blasted the mountain to carve the sculpture.

b. Mount Rushmore is in the Black Hills of South Dakota.

c. Theodore Roosevelt's face is carved on Mount Rushmore.

d. The carving of George Washington's face is sixty feet high.

Name _____ Date _____

# Identifying Investigation Needs and Making Plans

**Use this page to help make a plan for your group investigation.**

**These are things we already know about our topic:**

_____

_____

_____

_____

**Finding more information will help you confirm or revise your conjectures. These are things we still need to do or find out:**

_____

_____

_____

_____

_____

_____

**These are people who might be experts about our topic:**

_____

_____

_____

## Identifying Investigation Needs and Making Plans (continued)

There are several kinds of sources of information you could use in your investigation. In your groups, decide which kinds of sources in the chart below will give useful information for your inquiry. **For each source, check whether you think it would be useful or not useful.**

| Possible Sources | Useful | Not useful |
|---|---|---|
| Encyclopedias | | |
| Books | | |
| Magazines | | |
| Newspapers | | |
| Films or TV Shows | | |
| Interviews | | |
| Personal Observation | | |
| Museums | | |
| Internet Sites | | |
| Other Materials | | |

**For each source that you checked as useful above, write down specific titles, people, or places you could use as a source. Then, write how each will be useful.**

Title or Name of Source: _____

How this source will be useful: _____

_____

Title or Name of Source: _____

How this source will be useful: _____

_____

Title or Name of Source: _____

How this source will be useful: _____

Name _____ Date _____

# Writing a Thank-You Note

**Think**    **Audience: Who** will read your note?

_____

**Purpose: What** is your reason for writing the thank-you note?

_____

**Prewriting**    Use this graphic organizer to plan your thank-you note.

Heading

_____ **Greeting**

_____

_____

_____    **Body**

_____

**Closing** _____

**Signature** _____

**Address for Envelope**

## Revising   Use this checklist to revise your thank-you note.

- ☐ Did you write the reason for the thank-you note?
- ☐ Did you include all of the parts of a note?
- ☐ Do all of the sentences in each paragraph tell about the topic of the paragraph?
- ☐ Are the sentences in a clear order?
- ☐ Did you add variety by sometimes using pronouns instead of nouns?
- ☐ Does your thank-you note sound friendly and polite?

## Editing/Proofreading   Use this checklist to correct mistakes.

- ☐ Did you use periods in titles?
- ☐ Did you use parentheses when adding extra information?
- ☐ Did you use correct spellings?
- ☐ Did you capitalize the greeting and the closing?
- ☐ Did you capitalize proper nouns?
- ☐ Did you end each sentence with correct punctuation?

## Publishing   Use this checklist to get your thank-you note ready to send.

- ☐ Neatly rewrite or type a final copy.
- ☐ Address an envelope.

Name _____ Date _____

# Spelling

**Focus**

**Comparative adjectives** compare two or more people, things, or ideas; they end in -er.

**Superlative adjectives** compare more than two people, things, or ideas; they end in -est.

For words that end in silent e, drop the e before adding -er or -est.

For words that end in -y, change the y to i before adding -er or -est.

**/aw/** is spelled aw, au_, augh, ough, all, and al and makes the sound as in the word taught.

**Practice** Sort the spelling words under the correct heading.

Comparative Adjective

1. _____

Superlative Adjective

2. _____

/aw/ spelled aw

3. _____

4. _____

**Word List**

1. fall
2. caught
3. faster
4. August
5. talk
6. small
7. fought
8. yawn
9. bought
10. thinnest
11. hawk
12. taught
13. chalk
14. tall
15. auto

**Challenge Words**

16. squawk
17. happier

/aw/ spelled *au_*

**5.** _____

**6.** _____

/aw/ spelled *augh*

**7.** _____

**8.** _____

/aw/ spelled *ough*

**9.** _____

**10.** _____

/aw/ spelled *all*

**11.** _____

**12.** _____

**13.** _____

/aw/ spelled *al*

**14.** _____

**15.** _____

Name _____  Date _____

# Periods and Capitalization of Places

**Periods** sometimes show abbreviations, or groups of letters that stand for longer words.

- Use periods after the initials in people's names, at the end of abbreviated titles, and after some abbreviations.

- Mr. L. Cook will be back Mon., Jan. 16th.

**Capitalize** the names of places that are proper nouns.

- Capitalize the names of cities, states, countries, buildings, and parks.

- We stayed at Old Faithful Lodge in Yellowstone in Wyoming.

**Write *Yes* if the nouns are capitalized correctly. Write *No* if the nouns are capitalized incorrectly.**

**1.** Do crocodiles live in the sewers of new york city? _____

**2.** Monkeys sometimes come into San Salvador, the capital of El Salvador. _____

**Below is a list of ingredients. Put periods after any abbreviations.**

**3.** 1 gal of milk

**4.** 1 lb of flour

**Apply**  **Read the thank-you letter below. Capitalize places, and add periods.**

Dr. Theodore Hill

72 E plum Ave

miami, fl

33101

Dear Dr Hill:

Thank you for the talk you gave at my school in miami. It was interesting to learn about starting a business. I'm glad Ms Ramirez, our principal, asked you to come. I'd like to start a business when I'm older. Maybe between Aug 5 and 25, during my summer vacation, I can visit your business in ft. lauderdale. Thank you again, Dr Hill.

Sincerely,

J T Morgan

Name _____ Date _____

# Possible Sources

**Focus**

When doing research, you must choose sources of information. **Possible sources** include things such as books, encyclopedias, and Web sites.

Some sources are better than others. When you pick sources, follow steps like these:

- Read about the author. Do you think the author knows about this topic?

- If you use an article, make sure the magazine is known for good information.

- Think about whom the book, article, or Web site was written for.

- Check whether the author provides a bibliography.

- Check whether the Web site has won awards.

- Find out who made the Web site. Would that person or group have a reason to leave out some facts?

**Practice**

Decide whether each source below is a source of good information when investigating *money*. Write *Yes* if it is a good source. Write *No* if not.

**1.** An encyclopedia article about dogs _____

**2.** A book about starting your own business _____

**3.** A government Web site explaining the history of United States money _____

**4.** A magazine article about opening a savings account; it is in a well-known money magazine _____

 **Apply** Look at the list of sources below. Decide whether each will be helpful during your unit investigation. If it will be helpful, write how it will help.

| Source | Do you plan to use it? | If you plan to use it, explain one reason why. |
|---|---|---|
| Encyclopedias | | |
| Books | | |
| Magazines | | |
| Newspapers | | |
| DVDs and videotapes | | |
| Television | | |
| Interviews | | |
| Museums | | |
| Internet | | |

Study Skills • *Skills Practice 1*

Name _____ Date _____

# The /oi/ Sound/Spellings

**Focus**
- The /**oi**/ sound can be spelled *oi* in the middle of words. Example: c*oi*n
- /**oi**/ can also be spelled *oy* at the end of words. Sometimes *oy* is at the end of a syllable in the middle of a word. Example: *joy, loyal*

**Practice**  Read each sentence. Write a word that rhymes with the word in the box to complete the sentence.

1. | **joy** |  Tom loves to play with his

_____ metal detector.

2. | **foil** |  He holds it over sand, dirt,

and _____.

3. | **join** |  When it finds a dime or another

_____, it beeps.

4. | **choice** |  "I've found it!" Tom calls in a loud

_____.

5. | **soy** |  As a result, the _____

has found lots of lost money!

**Apply** Circle the correct spelling of each word to complete the sentences.

**6.** Benjamin Franklin lived in Boston as a small (boi/boy).

**7.** He wanted to (voiage/voyage) as a sailor.

**8.** But his brother (employed/emploied) him as a printer.

**9.** Franklin did not (toyl/toil) there for long.

**10.** He made the (choice/choyce) to work as a printer in Philadelphia.

**11.** He (enjoied/enjoyed) making new things.

**12.** The (poynt/point) of his lightning rod kept his house safe.

**13.** He made the first library, and it gave people much (joi/joy).

**14.** He talked to British (roials/royals) after the war.

**15.** He tried not to (annoy/annoi) them as he worked for peace.

**UNIT 3** Lesson 4

**Name** _____ **Date** _____

# Irregular Comparative and Superlative Adjectives

**Focus** Some **comparative** and **superlative adjectives** are **irregular.** This means they do not follow the rules.

- Irregular comparative and superlative adjectives do not add -er or -est.

| Adjective | Comparative | Superlative |
|-----------|-------------|-------------|
| good ⟶ | better ⟶ | best |

- They change spellings.

    The pond had <u>little</u> water.
    The bucket had <u>less</u> water.

**Practice** Choose a comparative adjective from the box to complete each sentence.

| farther | worse | more | better |
|---------|-------|------|--------|

**1.** I felt well yesterday, but today I felt even _____.

**2.** The bad milk can only be _____ today.

**3.** There were many ducks on the shore, but still

_____ on the pond.

**4.** The family had driven far, but they had

_____ to go.

**Apply** Choose a superlative adjective from the box to complete each sentence.

| worst | farthest | least | best |
| --- | --- | --- | --- |

**5.** Benny beat the other runners because he

ran the _____.

**6.** Josh did not finish his drink because it was the

_____ thing he had ever tasted.

**7.** The second apple is better than the first, but the

third is _____.

**8.** Of all the girls, Jin was the thirstiest because she

drank the _____.

**Read each group of sentences. Write a new sentence comparing the information. Use an irregular comparative or superlative adjective.**

**9.** Raquel has two marbles. Zoe has three.

_____

_____

**10.** Akna ran halfway across the field. Saabir ran to the end of the field.

_____

_____

Name _____ Date _____

# Selection Vocabulary

**Focus**

**factory** (fak' • tûr • ē) *n.* a building or group of buildings where things are made (page 319)

**hired** (hīûr • d) *v.* past tense of **hire:** to give a job to; to employ (page 319)

**managed** (man' • ijd) *v.* past tense of **manage:** to direct or control (page 319)

**secretary** (sek' • rə • tâ' • rē) *n.* a person whose job is to write letters and keep records for another person or a business (page 319)

**millionaire** (mil' • yə • nâr) *n.* a person who has money or property worth a million or more dollars (page 320)

**charged** (chärjd) *v.* past tense of **charge:** to ask a price (page 322)

**sued** (so͞od) *v.* past tense of **sue:** to start a case against in a court of law (page 322)

**wealth** (welth) *n.* riches (page 325)

**Practice** **Circle the word that matches each person, place, or thing.**

**1.** Robin keeps records for a law firm.
millionaire       secretary

**2.** Pencils are made in this building.
factory       wealth

**3.** Mr. Martin has a house worth two million dollars.
millionaire       secretary

**4.** The chest was full of gold coins.
factory       wealth

**Apply** The vocabulary words in the sentences below have been mixed up. Cross out the incorrect vocabulary word in each sentence. Write the correct one.

**5.** The play's director charged the actors and told

them where to move. _____

**6.** Dr. Evans was rich because he had a lot of sued.

_____

**7.** The workers at the secretary made cars.

_____

**8.** Mrs. Froman sued the boy and paid him

to cut her lawn. _____

**9.** The factory was a woman with millions

of dollars. _____

**10.** Bob charged the bus company in a court

of law. _____

**11.** The cashier hired the customer ten dollars.

_____

**12.** The principal asked her wealth to write a letter

for her. _____

**Name** _____ **Date** _____

# Things Worth More Than Money

Money is important both to the individual and to society, but it is not the most important thing. As you do your reading and investigations for this unit, record things that are more important than money.

I think _____

is more important than money because _____

_____

_____

I think _____

is more important than money because _____

_____

_____

## Things Worth More Than Money (continued)

I think _____

is more important than money because _____

_____

_____

I think _____

is more important than money because _____

_____

_____

I think _____

is more important than money because _____

_____

_____

Name _____ Date _____

# Writing an Invitation

**Think** | **Audience: Who** will read your invitation?

_____

**Purpose: What** is your reason for writing the invitation?

_____

_____

**Prewriting** | Use this graphic organizer to plan your invitation.

**Date:** _____

**Time:** _____

**Place:** _____

**Reason:** _____

**Notes:** _____

_____

**Address for Envelope**

## Revising    Use this checklist to revise your invitation.

☐ Does your invitation have all the information from the graphic organizer?

☐ Is the information organized in a way that is easy to understand?

☐ Did you choose clear and specific words?

☐ Does your invitation sound friendly?

## Editing/Proofreading    Use this checklist to correct mistakes.

☐ Did you spell names of people, places, and dates correctly?

☐ Did you write the correct address and zip code?

☐ Did you use apostrophes with possessive nouns?

☐ If you asked a question, did you end it with a question mark?

## Publishing    Use this checklist to get your invitation ready to send.

☐ Neatly rewrite or type a final copy.

☐ Add a map to show where the event will be.

Name _____ Date _____

# Spelling

**Focus**

**Irregular comparative** and **superlative adjectives** are not formed by adding -er or -est to the ends of the words. Sometimes comparatives and superlatives add the words *more* (comparative) or *most* (superlative) before the words being compared instead of adding the endings -er or -est.

**/oi/** is spelled *oi* and *_oy* and makes the sound as in the word *boy*.

**Practice**

**Sort the spelling words under the correct heading.**

Comparative adjectives

1. _____

2. _____

3. _____

Superlative adjectives

4. _____

5. _____

6. _____

**Word List**

1. better
2. royal
3. less
4. spoil
5. most
6. moist
7. voice
8. oyster
9. coin
10. best
11. joy
12. more
13. point
14. cowboy
15. least

**Challenge Words**

16. employer
17. worse

/oi/ spelled *oi*

7. _____

8. _____

9. _____

10. _____

11. _____

/oi/ spelled _*oy*

12. _____

13. _____

14. _____

15. _____

Name _____ Date _____

# The Articles *a* and *an*

**Focus**

The words **a** and **an** are articles. **Articles** are special adjectives that introduce nouns.

- The articles *a* and *an* are indefinite. This means they refer to a general person, place, thing, or idea.

- Use *an* when the noun following it begins with a vowel sound.

- I bought <u>a</u> bicycle helmet last week.

- <u>An</u> orange has a lot of vitamin C.

**Practice**  **Read each sentence below. If *a* and *an* have been used correctly, write *correct*. If not, write *incorrect*.**

**1.** Last week was an adventure because I camped.

_____

**2.** We hiked through an forest, and then we set

up a tent. _____

**3.** Each of us had an backpack with food.

_____

**4.** We planned to have an campfire, but it rained.

_____

**5.** Still, it was a lot of fun. _____

**Apply** **Write the correct article, *a* or *an,* in each blank.**

**6.** Wake up at _____ early hour.

**7.** Put on _____ warm coat and

_____ pair of boots.

**8.** Fix _____ egg for breakfast.

**9.** Wash out and carry _____
pail to the barn.

**10.** Fill the pail with _____ pound
of feed and give it to the cows.

**Read the paragraph below. Cross out any incorrect articles, and write the correct article.**

Yesterday I went to the zoo. I saw a elephant put

a pile of straw into its mouth. Nearby, a spider made

an big web in its cage. Dolphins swam, and a monkey

swung from an vine in the new monkey house. I even saw

a Bengal tiger. It was an fun visit, and all the animals

seemed happy.

Name _____ Date _____

# Graphs

**Focus**

A **graph** is a type of chart.

• Graphs show information in a small space. For example, a graph could show the number of rainy days in a city.

• Graphs can help compare and contrast. For example, a graph could show and compare the number of rainy days in three different cities.

• A graph can show a change over time. For example, a graph could show how rainfall changes from month to month.

• A title shows what type of information is in the graph. For example, the title **Sunny Days in Miami** tells that a graph will probably show how many sunny days there were in Miami.

• Horizontal (side-to-side) and vertical (up-and-down) titles show what is being compared or how much time has passed.

**Practice**
**Look at each graph title below. Decide if it will *compare* or *show a change over time.* Circle the correct choice.**

1. **The Number of Moons Orbiting Each Planet**
   This graph will probably
   **a.** compare. **b.** show a change over time.

2. **Growth of a Bay Tree**
   This graph will probably
   **a.** compare. **b.** show a change over time.

**Apply**   Study the graph. Fill in the circle next to the correct answer for each question.

**Favorite Pet**

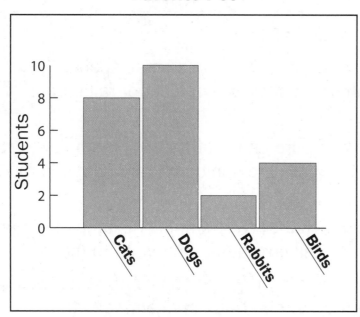

Based on a class poll of 24 students.

**3.** What is the title of the graph?
   ○ 24 students    ○ Favorite Pet    ○ Best Sport

**4.** How many students liked cats?
   ○ 2              ○ 4              ○ 8

**5.** How many students were in the class?
   ○ 8              ○ 24             ○ 10

**6.** What was the class's favorite pet?
   ○ birds          ○ rabbits        ○ dogs

**7.** What was the class's least favorite pet?
   ○ rabbits        ○ birds          ○ cats

**8.** How many students liked dogs?
   ○ 24             ○ 0              ○ 10

Name _____ Date _____

# Review of the /ō/, /ow/, /o͞o/, and /ū/ Sound/Spellings

**Focus**
- The /ō/ sound can be spelled *ow*. Example: *kn<u>ow</u>*
- The /**ow**/ sound can be spelled *ow*. Example: *n<u>ow</u>*
- The /o͞o/ sound can be spelled *ue*, *ew*, and *u_e*. Example: *f<u>ew</u>*
- The /ū/ sound can be spelled *ue*, *ew*, and *u_e*. Example: *val<u>ue</u>*

**Practice**    **Write a word from below that rhymes with each underlined word.**

| new | low | now |

**1.** Garage sale! Garage sale! Stuff to make you say <u>wow</u>!

Garage sale! Garage sale! Buy everything _____.

**2.** This stuff is fantastic. This stuff has got to <u>go</u>.

Take this cool older bike—the price is so _____.

**3.** Each book is a quarter. Buy a <u>few</u>.

These books are so cheap it's hard to believe they're _____.

 **Apply**  **Read each word below. Write *C* if it is spelled correctly. If it is not spelled correctly, write the correct spelling on the line.**

**4.** throoe _____

**5.** cow _____

**6.** bookends _____

**7.** toobe _____

**8.** choo _____

**9.** throw _____

**10.** value _____

**11.** snooe _____

**Read the news story below. Find the three spelling mistakes. Cross them out, and write the correct spellings.**

### Watch Out When Buying Used Bikes
by Owen Cook

At a flea market yesterday, Carrie thought she got a good valuu on the bike. She and her mother put it in the car without trying it. By the time she realized the chain was broken, it was too late.

"It looked like a coot bike," Carrie said. Her mother agreed. "And we were excited the price was so loa."

Unfortunately, this kind of thing happens a lot. People need to be careful when buying used toys and bikes. Test the item. Make sure the deal is as good as it sounds.

**Name** _____ **Date** _____

# Review of Inflectional Endings and Comparative and Superlative Adjectives

**Focus**

- For words that end in /a/, /e/, /i/, /o/, or /u/ and a consonant, double the final consonant before adding -ed or -ing.

  Example: tap, ta**pping**, ta**pped**

- For words that end with a silent e, drop the e before adding -ed or -ing. Example: type, typ**ing**, typ**ed**

- For words ending in *consonant + -y,* change the y to i before adding -ed. Example: study, stud**ied**

- Add -er to form regular comparative adjectives. For some longer adjectives, add *more.*

  Example: long**er**      **more** beautiful

- Add -est to form regular superlative adjectives. For some longer adjectives, add *most.*

  Example: long**est**      **most** beautiful

- Irregular comparative and superlative adjectives change spellings. They do not follow the rules.

  Example: good, better, best

**Practice** **Change each word into a comparative adjective.**

**1.** Change *fancy* into a comparative adjective. _____

**2.** Change *good* into a comparative adjective. _____

**UNIT 3** Lesson 5

**Change each word into an *-ed* or *-ing* word.**

**3.** Change *choose* into an *-ing* word. _____

**4.** Change *cut* into an *-ing* word. _____

**5.** Change *chop* into an *-ed* word. _____

**6.** Change *spend* into an *-ing* word. _____

**7.** Change *buy* into an *-ing* word. _____

**Use the words you made on this page and on the previous page to complete the sentences below.**

**8.** Your money can make the world _____ than it is.

**9.** For example, _____ down rain forests hurts Earth.

**10.** But some rain forests have been _____ down.

**11.** People use the wood to make _____, more expensive furniture and paper.

**12.** You can help by not _____ these products.

**13.** Ask questions when _____ what to buy.

**14.** Think about how you are _____ your money.

Word Structure • *Skills Practice 1*

Name _____ Date _____

# Selection Vocabulary

**Focus**

**county** (coun' • tē) *n.* part of a state (page 334)

**equipment** (ə • kwip' • mənt) *n.* tools and supplies used for a given purpose (page 335)

**segregation** (se • grə • gā' • shən) *n.* the practice of setting one group apart from another (page 337)

**unconscious** (un • kon' • shəs) *adj.* not awake (page 337)

**bundled** (bun • dəld) *v.* past tense of **bundle:** to wrap together (page 338)

**failing** (fāl' • ing) *adj.* losing money (page 340)

**stations** (stā' • shənz) *n.* plural form of **station:** a place where a service is performed (page 342)

**Practice**  **In writing with alliteration, two or more words begin with the same sound. Complete each alliterative sentence below with the correct vocabulary word.**

**1.** Ulmer was unable to wake up his _____ uncle.

**2.** The baker _____ the bumpy bread baskets.

**3.** Stylists soap hair at shampoo _____.

**4.** Colusa _____ is in California.

**5.** The _____ flying fish store was a flop.

**Apply**   Write *Yes* or *No* to answer each question below.

**6.** Is a *failing* store making lots of money? _____

**7.** Did some states have *segregation* years ago? _____

**8.** When you sleep, are you *unconscious*? _____

**9.** Could a gardener use gardening *equipment*? _____

**10.** Are *stations* parts of a state? _____

**11.** If someone *bundled* sticks together, are the sticks

tied in a group? _____

**12.** Is a *county* a place where people count money? _____

Name _____ Date _____

# Writing a News Story

**Audience: Who** will read your news story?

_____

**Purpose: What** is your reason for writing this news story?

_____

**Prewriting** Use this graphic organizer to plan your news story.

| The Five Ws |
|---|
| **Who** is involved in this story? |
| _____ |
| **What** happened? |
| _____ |
| **When** did the event take place? |
| _____ |
| **Where** did the event take place? |
| _____ |
| **Why** did the event happen? |
| _____ |

## Revising    Use this checklist to revise your news story.

☐ Does your headline tell about the subject of your story?

☐ Did you include a byline, lead, body, and ending?

☐ Did you cover the five *W*s in the lead?

☐ Did you include details and quotes in the body?

☐ Did you only cover facts?

## Editing/Proofreading    Use this checklist to correct mistakes.

☐ Did you spell names of people, places, and dates correctly?

☐ Is each paragraph indented?

☐ Did you capitalize proper nouns?

☐ Did you use correct punctuation?

## Publishing    Use this checklist to get your news story ready for publication.

☐ Neatly rewrite or type a final copy.

☐ Add a drawing or photograph that shows the story's subject.

Name _____     Date _____

# Spelling

**Focus** Remember:
/ō/ is spelled o, o_e, _ow, and oa_.
**/ow/** is spelled ou_ and ow.
**/o͞o/** is spelled oo, _ew, u_e, _ue, and u.
**/ū/** is spelled u, u_e, _ew, and _ue.

**Practice** Sort the spelling words under the correct heading.

/ō/ spelled o

1. _____

/ō/ spelled ow

2. _____

/ō/ spelled oa_

3. _____

/ow/ spelled ou_

4. _____

5. _____

**Word List**

1. glow
2. bonus
3. road
4. town
5. owl
6. pound
7. about
8. July
9. scoop
10. due
11. flew
12. use
13. rule
14. mule
15. unit

**Challenge Words**

16. county
17. tissue
18. raccoon

**/ow/** spelled *ow*

6. _____

7. _____

/$\overline{oo}$/ spelled *oo*

8. _____

/$\overline{oo}$/ spelled *_ew*

9. _____

/$\overline{oo}$/ spelled *u_e*

10. _____

/$\overline{oo}$/ spelled *_ue*

11. _____

/$\overline{oo}$/ spelled *u*

12. _____

/ū/ spelled *u*

13. _____

/ū/ spelled *u_e*

14. _____

15. _____

Name _____ Date _____

# Subjects and Predicates

**Focus**

The **subject** names who or what a sentence is about.

- A **simple subject** is the main word or words in a sentence. It is usually a noun or pronoun.

  My <u>mother</u> is a doctor.

- A **compound subject** has two or more simple subjects combined by a conjunction.

  <u>Tyrone</u> and <u>I</u> went horseback riding.

The **predicate** tells what the subject is or does.

- A **simple predicate** tells one thing about the subject.

  My sister <u>visits</u> her grandmother.

- A **compound predicate** tells two or more things about the same subject. They are connected by a conjunction.

  The zebras <u>eat</u> and <u>sleep</u> at the zoo.

**Practice**

Read each sentence. If the underlined words are two simple subjects, write *S*. If they form a compound subject, write *C*.

1. <u>Abraham Lincoln</u> was born in 1809, and <u>he</u> first

   lived in Kentucky. _____

2. Then <u>he</u> lived in Illinois, and <u>he</u> got married. _____

3. <u>Lincoln</u> and his <u>wife</u> moved when he became

   president. _____

**Apply**  **Read each sentence. If the underlined words are two simple predicates, write S. If they form a compound predicate, write C.**

**4.** Lincoln <u>read</u> and <u>thought</u>, and then he wrote many

speeches. _____

**5.** He <u>helped</u> slaves because he <u>thought</u> everyone

should be free. _____

**6.** The North <u>fought</u> and <u>won</u> the Civil War, and slavery

ended. _____

**Circle simple subjects. Underline compound predicates.**

Many Germans moved to Cincinnati in the 1800s.

They did not have much, and they wanted better lives.

They lived and worked near a waterway. They called it

"the Rhine," because they remembered the Rhine River in

Germany. The area was called Over-the-Rhine.

Many people could not buy homes, so they worked

and saved together. People gave money every week, and

then they drew straws. Whoever picked the right straw

got all the money. That person could build a house.

Name _____ Date _____

# Comparing Information Across Sources

> **Focus** Good writers use the most **reliable sources** they can find. When something is reliable, it means you can trust it. To make sure your source is reliable, ask yourself the following questions:
>
> - Is the source written by an expert? Book jackets and notes at the beginning or end of articles sometimes give information about the authors.
>
> - Is the source up-to-date? Would another source be more up-to-date?
>
> - Is the information detailed enough?
>
> - Does the information relate to your topic?

**Practice** Draw a checkmark beside each source you have used so far in your unit investigation. Circle any sources that you would like to use.

☐ almanac                 ☐ dictionary              ☐ atlas

☐ encyclopedias       ☐ books                     ☐ magazines

☐ newspapers          ☐ DVDs                      ☐ interviews

☐ personal experiences ☐ museums            ☐ Web sites

 **Apply** Think about your unit investigation. On the lines below, list the names of the sources that you are using. Write how you can check that each source is reliable.

**Source used:** _____

**How to check:** _____

_____

_____

**Source used:** _____

**How to check:** _____

_____

_____

**Source used:** _____

**How to check:** _____

_____

_____

**Source used:** _____

**How to check:** _____

_____

_____

**Name** _____ **Date** _____

# Proofreading Marks

¶       Indent

¶ Once upon a time, many years
ago, there lived a dinosaur
named Rocky. He lived . . .

∧       Add something.

a ∧ penny   *shiny*

⌿       Take out something.

Rabbits live in i⌿n burrows.

≡       Make a capital letter.

california
≡

╱       Make a small letter.

We go camping in ╱Summer.

sp       Check spelling.

sp (freind)

⊙       Add a period.

There are eight planets in the
solar system ⊙